THE SPIRIT OF BLACK HAWK

BOOKS BY JASON BERRY

The Spirit of Black Hawk

Lead Us Not Into Temptation:
Catholic Priests and the Sexual Abuse of Children

Up From the Cradle of Jazz:
New Orleans Music Since World War II
(with Jonathan Foose and Tad Jones)

Amazing Grace: With Charles Evers in Mississippi

The SPIRIT *of* BLACK HAWK

A Mystery of Africans and Indians

Jason Berry

UNIVERSITY PRESS OF MISSISSIPPI / JACKSON

Library of Congress Cataloging-in-Publication Data

Berry, Jason.
    The spirit of Black Hawk / Jason Berry.
        p.   cm.
    Includes bibliographical references and index.
    ISBN 0-87805-806-0 (cloth : alk. paper)
    1. Black Hawk, Sauk chief, 1767–1838 (Spirit)—Cult—Louisiana—
New Orleans.   2. Afro-American Spiritual churches—Louisiana—
New Orleans.   3. New Orleans (La.)—Church history—20th century.
I. Title.
BX6194.A4634N483   1995
289.9—dc20   95-20270
                                                                      CIP

British Library Cataloging-in-Publication data available

FOR ANDREW M. GREELEY,

with enduring gratitude

AND FOR SIMONETTE,

my sweet bright shining star

God is a spirit, and they that worship him
must worship him in spirit and in truth.
—John 4: 24

CONTENTS

ACKNOWLEDGMENTS

My primary debt is to members of the Spiritual church community in New Orleans, whose unfailing courtesy I hope this book in some way repays. The late Deacon Frank Lastie and his wife, Alice, were guides for Jonathan Foose and me in our television documentary work of 1979–80 and in the subsequent research for an earlier book, *Up From the Cradle of Jazz.*

I am grateful to Reverend Jules Anderson, who has since left New Orleans, for introducing me to the Black Hawk services.

Archbishop E. J. Johnson, pastor of the Israelite Divine Spiritual Church, has welcomed me to his services on numerous occasions, and to him I offer lasting thanks. I am also grateful to Bishop Edmonia Caldwell, Bishop Oliver Coleman and his wife, Bishop Efzelda Coleman, Bishop Inez Adams, and various church members.

The Louisiana Endowment for the Humanities awarded me a publication grant for the final phase of work; the LEH's predecessor, the Louisiana Committee for the Humanities, supported the video documentary sixteen years ago. Institutions such as LEH are a lifeblood for scholars and independent writers. A state as culturally rich as this one is fortunate to have Michael J. Sartisky as director of

LEH. To a high standard of probing scholarship Michael adds an intuitive sense of cultural dynamics. I count him as a trusted friend. I am also grateful to the LEH staff, particularly Kathryn A. Mettelka and Sandra Willis.

Academic interest in the Spiritual churches has grown in recent years. *The Spirit of Black Hawk* draws upon the work of scholars who shared information and personal reflections, aiding me immeasurably.

Photographer and historian Michael P. Smith, whose pioneering work in the 1970s exposed so many of us to the Spiritual community, gave a constructive reading of the chapter on Leafy Anderson, provided photographs, patiently answered questions large and small, and gave me several important leads. Mike is a rare cultural resource of New Orleans, and to him goes a large thanks.

Claude Jacobs and Andy Kaslow, authors of the first anthropological study of the local churches, were ever gracious in giving insights, providing documents and answering questions. In like measure, David Estes, associate professor of English at Loyola University of New Orleans, generously shared from his research and publications on the Spiritual churches.

Anthropologist Hans A. Baer of the University of Arkansas, Little Rock, author of the first major study of the Spiritual church movement, elucidated several key points and even sent me books.

To all of these men I reiterate my thanks.

I am deeply indebted to anthropologist Nancy Oestreich Lurie of Milwaukee who gave seasoned insights into the Black Hawk War, provided source citations that proved invaluable, and helped me understand Black Hawk in the time and setting in which he lived.

Photographer Syndey Byrd, whose color images accompany the text, is a long-standing friend and colleague with whom it is always a pleasure to work.

My first article on Black Hawk appeared in *New Orleans Magazine* in 1984, under editor Linda Matys, for whom I wrote often and with pleasure. My last article on the subject appeared in the same magazine, in December 1994, under editor Errol Laborde, a gentleman and scholar. The longest journalistic treatment I did was for the *Chicago Reader*, whose editor, Michael Lenihan, plunged into the Illinois and Wisconsin history, enriching the piece. A writer is lucky for such editors.

The Reverend Andrew M. Greeley responded to an early version of the *Reader* piece with great enthusiasm. In dedicating this book to Andy (and to my ten-year-old daughter, whom he gave a University of Chicago T-shirt) I express appreciation for his role in my previous work, a topic that exacted much from each of us.

Literary agent Don Congdon exerts a steady hand in my career, for which I am ever thankful.

JoAnne Prichard at the University Press of Mississippi jumped on the idea for this book the moment I mentioned it, and it has been rewarding to work with her, director Richard Abel and their colleagues. I am grateful to Anne Stascavage for the index.

For various favors: Richard B. Allen, Barbara Blaine, Lamar D. Berry, Mary Frances Berry, William Bertrand, Charles and Kent

Davis, Mark J. Davis, Tom Dent, William Ferris, Samuel A. Floyd, Jr., Jonathan Foose, John Glavin, Jeffrey Gillenkirk, Collin Hamer of the Louisiana Division of the New Orleans Public Library, Quin Hillyer, Allen Johnson, Jr., Lawrence Powell, Bruce Boyd Raeburn, curator of the William Ransom Hogan Jazz Archive at Tulane University, June Rosner, Nancy Sternberg, Robert Farris Thompson, writer Ben Sandmel, and Christine Walsh.

MOVEMENTS

OF THE SPIRIT

Rev. Jules Anderson holding Black Hawk service, photograph by
Michael P. Smith, 1980

M y first encounter with the spirit of Black Hawk came on the Friday night before Mardi Gras in 1979. Although I had visited other Spiritual churches in New Orleans, nothing foreshadowed the sheer drama of that night, the felt presence of such an otherworldly force.

It was a muggy February evening, with a warmth that made winter feel like summer. Webs of mist shrouded the city as I left the French Quarter, following Saint Claude Avenue, crossed the Industrial Canal bridge and headed into a threadbare black neighborhood of the lower Ninth Ward.

I was in the research stage of a television documentary about families of jazz musicians. The patriarch of one clan, a deacon in the Spiritual churches, told me of a ceremony invoking the spirit of Black Hawk, a deceased Indian leader. Black Hawk had little direct connection to my project, but curiosity hath its currents.

The mist had turned to rain when I reached the church, a small cement block building with the exterior structure of a former laundromat. Only a dozen people were inside; most were women. The interior resembled innumerable African-American chapels and churches in this or any southern city—framed pictures of Jesus, candles on a modest altar, an old creaky piano—but with one major difference. In front of the altar stood a teepee made of thin stakes, with incense burning at its base.

I introduced myself to the bishop, who had been expecting me, and after an exchange of amenities sat down in a rear pew.

After opening prayers and an a capella hymn punctuated by tambourine bursts from a woman seated near the altar, the bishop delivered a brief offertory. "And so," he said to the small flock, "we welcome tonight our Black Hawk celebrator . . ."

The man who would be Black Hawk wore a flowing white gown. He was about twenty-three, with olive-brown skin, dark hair and eyebrows and dark piercing eyes. His name, I later learned, was Jules Anderson. But that night, as far as I was concerned, he was Black Hawk.

"We come tonight to speak of a great warrior," he began, "the great chief—Black *Hawk!* And all of us know how Black Hawk will come to our aid. He will help you. He will *fight* your battles . . . if you just be still."

A bolt of thunder struck the sky, and the tiny chapel absorbed the current. Thunder hit again: rain started pounding the roof like cannonballs. Out went the lights. I was the only white there that night, and with heavy rain shaking the church, now engulfed in darkness, I felt an eery sensation—as if the sudden pull of the young preacher's words and his loose-limbed gesticulations were somehow certifying the presence of a higher power.

In 1971, as a political activist, I had visited several score black churches in rural Mississippi, and since then had spent enough time in the gospel-soaring churches of New Orleans to feel at ease when others articulated their belief through varied ceremonies. But this ritual, I felt, was strange.

Anderson's robe shone a spectral white in flickering lights of candles on the altar. "Remember that Black Hawk will help you! He's here to *use* his powers! We call to him, we pray to him, we tell him what we need."

Just then the door to the church flew open and volleys of rain blew in. All heads turned. A man in his early twenties stood there, soaking wet and somewhat dazed. The bishop emerged from darkness beside the altar, and, as an overhead light came on, he seemed to sense trouble. The newcomer, with eyes red as coals, was lit up on something.

"We welcome all our people," the bishop murmured cautiously.

Anderson paused at the altar, waiting for the word to resume. "We pray for those behind bars," intoned the bishop. "We offer counsel and friendship to those in the night."

"It's rainin' hard, y'all," blurted the newcomer.

The bishop escorted the man to an empty pew and whispered to him as he sat. For a moment, seeing the furrowed brow of an elderly woman, I sensed embarrassment—that on the night a white visitor should come, a drugged man would interrupt the service. But she turned toward the altar, and I thought how presumptuous it was of me to imagine she had thought that at all.

The lights lowered once again. Rain continued drumming the roof. I noticed now the small wooden statue of an Indian, which had been placed on the altar just behind the teepee. Smoke curled up amidst the incense.

"We believe in the spirits," Anderson said, "and we know the spirits will come if we call them."

"Yes, Lawd!" cried a woman.

The sky exploded again, shooting a chill up my spine. Anderson paced back and forth in front of the teepee.

"The name *Bea*trice!" he said. "The name *Bea*trice has come to me. Beatrice . . . *who is Beatrice?*"

From the man just arrived came the words: "That's my momma, bra!"

All heads turned as Anderson pointed to the stranger. "Yeah, and yo' momma's *worried* about you! She's walkin' up and down, pacin' the floor. She knows you gone out in the streets, and *all kinda* things can happen! Look at you: you *know* yo' momma's worried. Beatrice is grieving!"

The man looked shocked. Then he said, "I wanna testify!"

"No," said the bishop calmly, from his seat behind the altar. "You can do that later on."

The man sat down, mumbling to himself.

"And we know from Black Hawk that we have to be careful about—our money," continued the celebrant. "We have to use our money carefully. Can't waste money. And you—" his voice was gentler now, as he faced a little lady in the front pew—"I know you been worried about money."

She nodded.

"And you *need* money."

"Yes-lawd," she said softly.

"All right now. The money is coming. But you have to wait. But the money *is* coming. Now, when the money comes, it will be a check in the mail. And you leave that check up on yo' bureau. When it comes, no matter how much you need that money, you leave it on the bureau, and wait five days before you spend it."

As he went through the room, addressing individuals, telling people to be patient, to plan this, not to worry about the relative who is sick or "the one who is so close to you . . . and yet, oh *so* far," it was clear that his prophecies were not the stuff of miracles. A folk preacher, he probably knew most of the people there, and in a congregation so small and so poor, advice on love or coping with financial stress was of a general, if intuitive, nature.

But the way he faced his followers, and the personal address to each of them elevated this general line of oratory into something more specific, and at the same time, charismatic. His sway over the tiny group was total. The man radiated confidence. In the Marshall McLuhan parlance he was media-hot. But how much of him was legit? Then again, in a room of true believers, who was I to doubt the function of his ministry?

As for Beatrice—well, if he didn't know the whacked-out dude, maybe he knew his mother, or at least knew of them. Then again, perhaps he had something of a gift, as faith most certainly is. The guy off the street was spellbound.

As the ceremony wore on, the chants to the Indian—"Black Hawk is a *watchman*! He will *fight* your battles!"—melded into a positive theme of reenforcement, a common struggle of solidarity. As he sang praises of Black Hawk I saw this ceremony as a performance of spirit: Anderson became the presence of Black Hawk, dancing across the floor, chanting, kneeling before the teepee, calling Black Hawk's name, making his spirit live.

The ritual reached a lull.

Back on his feet, Anderson again was pacing the floor. "Now, I ain't gonna call any names, but there is money in this room . . . *Big money!*"

The budget for the video documentary on which I was at work had just been awarded in a grant from the Louisiana Committee for the Humanities: thirty-six thousand dollars. When he said, "There is big money in this room," my thoughts went *chink* like a cash register: thirty-six thousand dollars, thirty-six thousand dollars . . .

"And the important thing about the money," he said, "is it got to be used *right*."

Anderson now stood at the altar holding candles sheaved in red glass bottles with a yellow Indian sticker stamped on each one. He was selling them for a dollar. He also sold small vials of a sweet-smelling oil. I stood in line with the others and purchased one of each. When everyone was back in the pews, Anderson began hitting his tambourine, chanting softly, and in the middle of this he stopped and pointed at me.

"If you want to know Black Hawk then you must come to the altar," he declared.

So, I went to the altar.

Anderson was pounding the tambourine harder as the rain continued its percussive currents on the roof. A woman in the front pew hit her tambourine as Anderson began dancing around the altar, everyone clapping in rhythm with his feet. Rather than look like a dumb cluck, I started dancing too, sort of, making a wide arc behind the celebrant and then slipping back into my seat, as he continued dancing and chanting.

I had never seen anything remotely like this. The Catholicism of my youth was considerably more understated.

As the documentary production moved into high gear, my coproducer, Jonathan Foose, arranged to videotape a ceremony at the Guiding Star Church under Deacon Frank Lastie. The documentary focussed on two of the city's musical families: the Neville Brothers, four rhythm-and-blues siblings on the road to stardom, and the Lasties, a lesser-known yet much-accomplished clan of the lower Ninth Ward. At seventy-nine, Deacon Lastie was a true jazz patriarch. Three of his sons—Melvin, David and Walter—had become professional jazzmen, while daughter Betty Ann was a wondrous gospel singer. (Melvin Lastie, a trumpeter, died in 1972. Walter, a drum-

Deacon Frank Lastie at Guiding Star Spiritual Church, photograph
by Michael P. Smith, 1973

mer, died in 1980 and David, a saxophonist, in 1987. Deacon Lastie has since died as well.)

In Deacon Lastie's home I had seen the Spiritual shrine Mrs. Alice Lastie had made, with an Indian figurine nestled among the bottles and glasses. Mrs. Lastie had spoken of an unnamed Indian to whom she prayed to help her oldest son, Melvin, on a trip to New York early in his career.

Each Spiritual church has a pantheon of saints, reflected in the icons, pictures, statues, and figures upon the altar. Although Black Hawk services were not a mainstay of the Guiding Star, the Indian persona figured prominently in the church and lives of Lastie's flock. When I broached the possibility of a Black Hawk segment in the film, Deacon Lastie was amenable. He also invited Jules Anderson.

There are roughly one hundred Spiritual churches in New Orleans, many of them quite small. Black Hawk is the most exotic saint in the Spiritual pantheon, holding equal status with such Catholic figures as Saint Michael the Archangel, Saint Joseph (father of Jesus, husband of Mary), Saint Daniel, Saint Benedict, and Queen Esther of the Old Testament, among others in these sectarian churches. The Spiritual religion took root in New Orleans about 1920.

Our focus for the documentary was the musical lineage begun with Deacon Lastie's drumming in the churches in the 1920s, a current that carried down the bloodline via his sons and daughter into a third generation, with grandsons Joseph "Fish" Lastie, Jr., and Herlin Riley—both in their twenties, both drummers.

As we prepared the church with lights, audio gear and a maze of wires, members of the congregation began filling the pews. Next to the podium, an Indian statue sat on a table covered with a white cloth and rows of oranges, apples, pears, and, at each end, grapefruits with their green stems. Behind the podium stood a three-tiered altar—one level with glass-encased candles, the second with statuettes of Mary and Joseph, separated by a vase of flowers, and on the top row a small statue of Jesus. The back wall, covered with a red curtain, had several religious pictures, including one of the Last Supper directly above the statue of Jesus. In the right-hand corner of the wall, an oversized replica of an old-fashioned door key was diagonally pointed down.

Deacon Lastie's mentor had been Mother Catherine Seals, a faith healer who settled in the lower Ninth Ward. In 1927, when Frank returned from Chicago, where he had hustled money as a pool shark, she redirected his life. Some members grumbled about the reverend mother taking a worldly young man under wing, but Lastie, who had learned drumming with Louis Armstrong in the Colored Waifs Home in 1913, carried a convert's zeal, and at Mother Catherine's suggestion, he began playing drums in church. "I endured the rebukes and scorns," he said in his sermon. "Now, they're very few churches that don't have a drum." In 1928 she baptized him. "I saw her perform so many miracles. I mean I've never seen anything like that in all the days of my life! The people she healed through the power of prayer."

Born in Kentucky in 1887, Catherine Seals arrived in New Orleans at age sixteen and began working as a domestic. She became a disciple of Mother Leafy Anderson, who founded the Spiritual religion in New Orleans; in 1922 Catherine suffered a paralytic stroke. A white faith healer whose help she sought refused to pray with her because she was black. The power of her own praying, legend has it, improved Catherine's health, and a vision inspired her to help others, regardless of race.

In 1928 a young writer named Zora Neale Hurston spent several months in New Orleans, gathering Negro folklore in an anthropological study. "Mother Catherine was not converted by anyone," she wrote. "Like Christ, Mohammed, Buddha, the call just came. No one stands between her and God."

> After the call, she consecrated herself by refraining from the sex relation, and by fasting and prayer.
> She was married at the time. Her husband prayed two weeks before he was converted to her faith. Whereupon she baptised him in the tub in the backyard. They lived together six months as a holy man and woman before the call of the flesh made him elope with one of her followers.

Sixty years ago the lower Ninth Ward was a semirural area straddling the Mississippi, downriver from the city proper. People hunted rabbit and possum in the fields; drainage was poor, and some parts were prone to flooding. Mother Catherine acquired land with the help of her followers and gave shelter to the homeless. "Her compound is called the Manger and is dedicated to the birth of children in or out of wedlock," wrote Hurston. The facility became a magnet for innumerable poor people. With room for three hundred worshipers, it became known as The Temple of the Innocent Blood. She decorated it with artworks of her own making—hand-painted statues, banners, stations of the cross, and hundreds of oil-burning lamps. Hurston wrote:

> She might have been the matriarchal ruler of some nomad tribe as she sat there with the blue band about her head like a coronet; a white robe and a gorgeous red cape falling away from her broad shoulders, and a box of shaker salt in her hand like a rod of office . . . All during her sermons the two parrots were crying from their cages. A white cockatoo would scream when the shouting got too loud. Three canary birds were singing and chirping happily all through the service. Four mongrel dogs strolled about. A donkey, a mother goat with her kid, numbers of hens, a sheep—all wandered in and out of the service without seeming out of place. A Methodist or Baptist church—or one of any denomination whatever—would have been demoralised by any of these animals. Two dogs found a place beside the heater. Three children under three years of age played on the platform in the rear without distracting the speaker or the audience. The blue and red robed saint stood immobile in her place directly behind the speaker and the world moved on.

When she died in 1930, at forty-three, a huge thunderstorm throttled the city. "The day of the funeral there were thousands of people," Deacon Lastie recalled. "Mother Catherine always said there'd come a day when the sun would shine in the rain. . . . When [the funeral] reached Industrial Canal bridge, the sun broke through and people started *fallin' out* on the bridge. People had *babies* in their arms, and they knew it was prophecy. That was a powerful, powerful woman and she done so much for people."

In a history of the New Orleans churches, anthropologists Claude J. Jacobs and Andrew J. Kaslow report that Mother Catherine's estate, with a value of somewhere between thirty-five hundred and four thousand dollars, had debts of nearly two thousand. "Various members were accused of having spent the late leader's money, so that the church, unable to meet its financial obligations, was forced to auction large parts of the group's property to pay the bills. The remaining members reorganized, and changed the name of the church to 'True Light,' but failed to attract a following the size of Mother Catherine's."

A line of reverend mothers, bishops and deacons had kept the Spiritual churches alive, if diffuse, in the decades following Mother Catherine's death. How Black Hawk fit into all this was still unclear to me on that spring evening in 1979 when Deacon Lastie introduced the young Reverend Anderson as "our Black Hawk *demonstrator.*"

He came to the podium rattling his tambourine in a counter-rhythm to Walter Lastie's drumming, chanting the words *"Black Hawk is a watchman"*—with people in the pews calling back the refrain—*"He's on the wall!"*

Against the backdrop of a red curtain his white robes stood out as if in bas-relief. He squared himself at the podium and began his sermon, expanding the idea of a historical presence by reading passages taken from a book, giving details of the real Black Hawk: a leader of the Sauk Indians in Illinois and Wisconsin who had led a rebellion against white soldiers and settlers in the 1830s. "You know Black Hawk was a man, he believed in togetherness," said Anderson, gesturing with a handkerchief, drawing his hands close. "He came together with—his people. And he believed in *standing up for his right!*"

"*Well, yessss!*" came the believers.

"And this is what Black Hawk is about—*righteousness!*"

"Yes, Lawd!"

"Show you how the spirit works: and Black Hawk is a great worker—"

"*Yes he is,*" said a man in a pew.

"If you're having a problem and you need justice, you take Black Hawk with you."

"*My my my!*"

"Take Black Hawk with you and tell God to *back up the spirit!*"

"*Wellll, yesss!*" cried a woman as a tambourine jangled.

"You know God put a deaf ear to man!"

"*Whoa, yesss!*"

"He said Jesus said I'm gonna pray to the Father. And the Father's gonna send you a *comforter*, which is the—"

"*—Holy Ghost!*"

"And you know when they tell me that one day the Holy Ghost assemble on John's *shoulder*, in the symbol of a *dove*—" he swept his hand across his chest, touching the handkerchief on his shoulder—"and any time it can work through a *dove* it oughta be able to work through somebody else!"

"*Amen!*"

"And *remember!*—that Black Hawk is a watchman. And he will *fight ya battles!* Fight your battles—"

"*Yes Lawd!*"

"—if you just be still . . . "

From the sermon I gathered a complex theological image of Black Hawk as a superheroic figure, equal parts history and myth, in whom impoverished black folk beheld a guardian. But Anderson made the spiritual persona more problematic in an ironic remark about his ministry, saying: ". . . and ever since then, I been making *big money* sellin' Black Hawk statues!"

In the weeks that followed, as we edited the film, the Black Hawk sequence proved daunting. Was the line about selling statues the Freudian slip of a huckster, or a naive admission about the commercial prowess of an Indian to whom poor people prayed? In the end, we decided not to use the statue-selling statement, as the Black Hawk segment was barely two minutes and including the remark would have required an interview to give viewers a more three-dimensional sense of Jules Anderson, who was a minor figure in one sequence of an hour-long documentary.

A music history book grew out of the documentary production and pulled me away from questions raised by the Black Hawk service. One afternoon in the fall of 1983, however, with work on the book nearly done, I bumped into Anderson on the street, and he agreed to do an interview. On October 29 I went to the house where he stayed on Elysian Fields.

The flamboyant young preacher was spending three days a week in Jeanerette, a town in Cajun country where he had a small Spiritual church. His mother had come from British Honduras, he said, which explained his dark Latin looks, and her grandmother, he insisted, had lived to be 135 years old. He told me that the Spiritual church where his father was minister, in a black Creole neighborhood, did not include Black Hawk in its pantheon of saints.

As a teenager Jules had left his father's church and joined the Church of God in Christ, which cleaved to a more conservative doctrine. "In my house I had an altar, saints on my altar and burning candles," he said. "This church did not agree with candle-burning, incense, statues, saints. Some of the elders came to my house and saw the altar; they said that this was not God. They cursed at me for having it, and I went through this thing, and I didn't know anything about Black Hawk at the time.

"So I prayed, and I went through this sensational experience I never had before," he continued. "It was like a voice, and a hand, and I actually seen my spirit leave my body. It was like a cloudy city, but it was one of the most beautiful things to see. I've never seen nothing similar to it, and they had these arches, and these people—I don't know if they was people or statues—but there were different kinds, Indians and others I had never seen. I heard a voice. It spoke to me. 'These are my saints and I will teach you how to use every one.' But the one that stuck with me out of all those was Black Hawk."

Not long after that, he said, "I was walking down the street in the French Quarter and this big Indian guy just came to me, in the spirit. It wasn't a real man. He was an Indian but he was dressed in ordinary American clothes, and he walked to me and folded his hands, like we see the statue of Black Hawk in Illinois. And he just walked right into me, and it was like a possession type thing I went into. And it was from that day on that I began to have this personal relationship with the spirit of Black Hawk, and I started to go around to different churches and other leaders told me I had the spirit strong. They said Black Hawk would work with me beautifully."

I had come to see the Spiritual churches as an extension of African cultural memory—celebrating those long dead as dynamic presences in the life of the flock, like ancestral shades in an animist tribe. Black Hawk was one spirit in a pantheon that borrowed from Catholicism, Voodoo, Protestantism, and the churches' own deceased ministers. The spirits are specific personalities called down from heaven to confer strength and resilience upon the believers through a drama of worship.

"Black Hawk is a spirit guide," Anderson continued, "and he is a warrior. He don't stand for any foolishness. When I was dealing with Black Hawk in a more constant way, I had an attitude that I didn't have to take anything, you know. I felt like I could fight for what I wanted and win. And I did that because I was totally into Black Hawk and it was good to an extent. But then I found it wasn't beneficial to me as a minister because of the basic fight: some churches do not invoke the spirit of Black Hawk. I had a reputation of being known only as Black Hawk.

"I don't believe in spirit *worship*," he said, checking himself in midthought. "I believe in spirit honor. Because by being a Christian it would be wrong to worship Black Hawk or any saint. They're not to be worshipped; they're to be entertained, to be welcomed, to be given praise. I'm a firm believer that we should worship only God. But a lotta folks cannot do anything unless the spirit of God will loosen the spirit. That's why a lot of people turn away from Black Hawk; they're making Black Hawk out to be a God."

A spirit guide is a role model and a medium who channels spiritual power into a minister or celebrants at a service. In essence, the spirit uses the believer as a vessel, stirring energies of a zone within the mind, often driving the believer into trance-like possessions or singing accompanied by wild dancing.

"I feel that Black Hawk has always been a part of the black spirit," explained Anderson. "We was took from Africa and that left us—we didn't hear any of those drums. It was the Indians that brought us back to the drums and the music. You could go on a Carnival day and see people full of Indian spirits [meaning blacks who parade in brightly feathered costumes, the Mardi Gras Indians]. You wouldn't know if you was in a Black Hawk service or an Indian rehearsal. Those people experience a spirit take-over."

He spoke of a chilling spirit visitation, in which a man's voice had entered his thoughts, telling him "the money's over the door," and when he revealed this to a woman he was counseling she understood immediately. The voice Anderson had heard, he explained, was that of a man she had known who had been murdered "over somethin' having to do with drugs . . . And she went home and found seven thousand dollars over the transom of a door in the house."

"Did she give you any money?"

"No," he said, frowning. "She could have given something for the role I played," he added with a wan smile.

Spiritual phenomena were part of his ministry, part of his life. He spoke of the spirits as forces circulating in a world that needed intercessors and mediums through whom the messages would find voice and presence.

"I feel that people are not aware because they are not spirit-educated. Folks have not taught them the difference between spirits. They feel that any Indian spirit that come in is Black Hawk and that is not true." Other Indian spirits that circulated included those of Sitting Bull and Running Water, he maintained.

He mentioned a man who had a Black Hawk altar in his home and wanted to use the spirit to take retribution on someone. "I refused to let him believe that he was invoking Black Hawk. And he actually passed out after [he tried]. I told him, 'You was not invoking Black Hawk' . . . because Black Hawk is a spirit of justice. You can't just send Black Hawk out here to hurt somebody. It's not the man you read about. He was a man for justice. You cannot take and make him be what he was not."

Black Hawk, he added, "was unable to accomplish all that he

wanted but his spirit is still, every day, giving justice to folks by the hundreds."

"What about Sitting Bull?" I asked, wondering how much of this to take in.

"Sitting Bull we know as a medicine man," he said matter-of-factly. "He's a good spirit to use for wisdom and patience. And some things, in life, we need to take time and sit down and think about them. And use our wisdom after we thought about it. Sitting Bull is a very good spirit for that . . . The old folks [used to] say 'I'm gonna be still and move at God's command.' And that's the way we invoke the spirit of Sitting Bull.

"A spirit is here to serve you," he continued. "In other words, if I serve the spirit that means that I'm not gonna be used. [But] if I let the spirit take control of me totally, I'm gonna start acting like that spirit in everything I do. Eventually my personality, my talk, my way of doing is not going to be like myself, it's going to be like a spirit. And I don't think the spirit is supposed to be with a person all that time. Because—face it, our everyday lives are not in the spirit . . . People that get caught up into that, and live this everyday life—and it becomes quite confusing."

BLACK HAWK

IN HISTORY

Portrait of Black Hawk, painting by George Catlin; courtesy of the National Museum of Art, Smithsonian Institution, gift of Mrs. Joseph Harrison, Jr.

I was born at the Sac Village, on Rock River, in the year 1767."
Thus begins *Life of Ma-Ka-Tai-Me-She-Kia-Kiak or Black Hawk*, the autobiography that the Indian dictated to a government interpreter in 1834.

In the past, some chroniclers of Indian history questioned the authenticity of Black Hawk's autobiography, which was reprinted several times after its initial publication. But Donald Jackson, a scholar who wrote an essay and footnotes for the most recent edition, published in 1955 by the University of Illinois Press, made a persuasive case that it is genuine. The interpreter, Antoine LeClaire, was a government Indian agent who spoke Black Hawk's tongue and read the dictated work back to him. (A newspaperman, John Patterson, published the work after editing it, and then republished his own version of the book years later, adding information that Jackson felt was suspect.) Although the original work is dotted with anglicisms, like "whilst," and phrases that betray a white man's pen, such embellishments recede beneath the power of the narrator's voice.

"Black Hawk's story," writes Donald Jackson, "despite the intrusive hands of interpreter and editor, is basically a tale told by an Indian from an Indian point of view."

It is a tale of betrayal, anger and humiliation. Black Hawk's force of character imbues the narrative with a sense of moral urgency—it marks the last gasp of Native American resistance to the white man's usurpation of the Northwest Territory, and the removal of resident Indian tribes from Illinois.

The village of Saukenak, which lay at the site of the present city of Rock Island, was located near the confluence of the Rock River and the Mississippi. The village covered about eight hundred acres; the Indians farmed corn, beans, squash, pumpkins and tobacco, and raced horses in the outlands. They lived in bark houses, and followed the calendar with dances that were part of their religious rites.

Forging a union with one branch of the beleaguered Fox tribe, the Sauk (also spelled Sac) became allies of the British in their battles with Americans over control of lands in southern Canada, Wisconsin and Illinois. Theirs was not a peaceful life, to judge from the Indian's memoir and historians' accounts of the Black Hawk War.

After mentioning his birth and giving a brief history of his ancestors, including how they came to occupy their village, Black Hawk vaults ahead in time to when he was about fifteen and took part in a bloody battle with the Osage Indians, a persistent enemy of the Sauk: "Standing by my father's side, I saw him kill his antagonist, and tear the scalp from his head. Fired with valor and ambition, I rushed furiously upon another, smote him to the earth with my tomahawk— run my lance through his body, took off his scalp, and returned in triumph to my father. He said nothing, but looked pleased. This was the first man I killed! . . . Our party then returned to our village, and danced over the scalps we had taken. This was the first time that I was permitted to join in a scalp-dance."

In a subsequent battle with the Cherokees, Black Hawk's father was killed. "I blacked my face, fasted, and prayed to the Great Spirit for five years—during which time I remained in a civil capacity, hunting and fishing." When the Osages attacked his tribe, Black Hawk counterattacked. "Their forces being so weak, I thought it cowardly to kill them"—instead he took them as prisoners. The sense of mercy is notable. Black Hawk was a warrior whose memoir emphasizes the number of men, and in some cases women and boys, he killed in battles with warring tribes. Yet he expresses a recurrent quest for justice, sometimes a *cri du coeur*, over the white man's ways.

Warfare was not the primary activity of the Sauk and Fox who lived on Rock Island. Groups of warriors answered to a chiefs' council. Ironically, Black Hawk himself was not a chief; rather he became a rebel from the power hierarchy of his tribe.

The Indians lived by seasonal rhythms. From October through May, bands of braves moved upriver, hunting fur, trapping beaver, trading pelts with Europeans and Americans. In warm months the people planted corn and other crops in the village environs. They also hunted buffalo on the prairie.

"Hunting grounds during the fur trade era were thus treated in some respects like capital property owned by a corporation," writes Anthony F. C. Wallace in a probing account of the economic and political forces preceding the war with the white forces.

Black Hawk with five other Sauk and Fox prisoners, painting by George Catlin; courtesy of the National Gallery of Art, Washington D.C.

For economic as well as environmental reasons, the chiefs' council monitored use of the land and regulated the volume of hunting. In 1804, the Sauk and Fox sold furs worth sixty thousand dollars in St. Louis. Such commerce brought new standards of living to the Indians. Supplanting primitive tools were steel knives, guns, kettles, needles—and alcohol, which was abused by white men as well as by Indians. "But," notes Wallace, "a crucial difference existed: the Indians of the frontier culture, orderly as they might be (except when drunk), were part of no larger organization; whereas white frontiersmen, however lawless, were part of a vast organization which could bring to bear in their behalf overwhelming economic and military force"—that is, the federal, state and territorial governments.

The Sauk-Fox lands extended well beyond Rock Island into parts of what are now Wisconsin, Iowa and Illinois. Lead mining was another staple of the Indians' economy. In the early 1800s, the federal government began to broker treaties among warring Indian nations of the upper Midwest. Enclosing the Indians geographically and tightening boundaries of those areas was part of a strategy to expand white settlement lands. This was especially so in territorial Wisconsin, where lead mines were opening.

In 1804 three white settlers near St. Louis were ambushed and killed by Sauk hunters. A young chief was identified and accused of murder. Black Hawk remarks that "one of our people killed an American." Wallace writes that four Sauk hunters murdered "some white settlers who were trespassing on Indian hunting lands" in vengeance over close ties between the white community and rival Osage warriors, and that "the act seems also to have been an attempt by a rebellious party of warriors to force the hand of their conciliatory chiefs."

According to Wallace, when the hunters returned to the Sauk community, they carried the scalps to the chiefs' council, telling them, "Now you that make the land to smile, go cry with the whites." As word of the killings spread, four Sauk bands living downriver from Rock Island fled their settlements in fear of retaliation by the whites. Two Sauk chiefs headed to St. Louis where they found a siege atmosphere, with whites making ready for war; the Indians denounced the murder and asked how they could make reparations. They returned to their community with a summons from Governor William Henry Harrison for a meeting with the chiefs' council—and a demand to produce the killers.

Unbeknownst to the Sauk envoys, the United States government had designs on greater areas of land under tribal control, which Harrison was under orders to obtain. The village council at Rock Island sent an accused young chief to Saint Louis with a delegation intent on "paying for the person killed," in Black Hawk's words—"thus covering the blood, and satisfying the relations for the man murdered." The discrepancy between the stories—a single victim and sole murderer, or several men who killed others—suggests confusion over what actually transpired.

Regardless, the situation played into the governor's hands: a treaty agreement would be exchanged for the warrior accused of murder. The Indians wanted assurance that their trade would not fall victim to war. Black Hawk himself was not part of the delegation. He tells us that the Sauk contingent, who returned from St. Louis wearing fine coats and medals (which were highly valued by Indians), reported that the American chief who met them wanted land "on the west side of the Mississippi, and some on the Illinois side" in exchange for the prisoner. They had agreed to the terms and signed a treaty—but had done so before the young chief escaped from the stockade and was shot dead by a guard.

President Thomas Jefferson's letter pardoning the Indian for killing settlers in self-defense came too late.

It was also too late to undo the treaty. Worse yet, according to Black Hawk, the Indians "had been drunk the greater part of the time they were in St. Louis."

The degree to which they drank also remains unclear. But Black Hawk's impression of the land deal as a swindle is borne out by the historical record. The Indians gave away a huge amount of land, including several villages, as part of an agreement that offered little more than promises to improve methods of trade and to resolve grievances—a pact the Indians considered necessary to halt white retribution for the murdered settlers.

Without a full complement of Sauk and Fox leadership present, the 1804 treaty ceded control of 15 million acres to the federal government, including a large area in upper Illinois and valuable lead mines in Wisconsin, in exchange for $2,234.50 and an annual payment by the government of $1,000. Annuities usually lasted thirty or forty years.

A telling clause stipulated that "as long as the lands" remained government property, "the Indians belonging to the said tribes shall enjoy the privilege of living or hunting on them." The unwritten message was that when settlers arrived, the Indians would have to vacate. As a result many Indians began leaving the area.

Black Hawk, described by historian Reuben Thwaites as an "obstinate patriot," resisted, and, along with other warriors and their families, stayed on Rock Island. To them the treaty was a fraud, despite its acceptance by chiefs desirous of peace.

Black Hawk's group was among those who came to be known as "the British band," for, unlike most Indians in the area, including the majority of his own tribe, Black Hawk sided with the British against the Americans in the War of 1812 and remained loyal to the British long after the waning of their influence in the region. This friendship made Black Hawk forever suspect in the eyes of American settlers and their government.

"He passionately hated the Americans," wrote Thwaites in a history of Wisconsin, "because they annoyed him, because the marauders of our nationality had stolen his property, because he had once been beaten by one of them, because they were intruders on the domains of his people, because his English father [the term Indians used for leader] hated them, because his rivals were their friends."

As Black Hawk told Antoine LeClaire, in his memoir: *"I had not discovered one good trait in the character of the Americans that had come to the country! They made fair promises but never fulfilled them!*

Whilst the British made but few—but we could always *rely upon their word!*

"Why did the Great Spirit ever send the whites to this island, to drive us from our homes, and introduce among us *poisonous liquors, disease and death?* They should have remained upon the island where the Great Spirit first placed them." [All italics appear in the text.]

On a trip to Madison, Black Hawk and his braves watched soldiers who had come in keelboats cut timber and build a fort, where, the Indians were told, they would be able to buy goods at low cost. But a momentum of mistrust was building. In the search for new hunting grounds, the Sauk roamed into territories of other tribes, triggering skirmishes. In an attack upon the fort, Black Hawk says he fired a shot through the rope that hoisted the flag at the garrison.

As white settlers came ever closer to fulfilling what they would later call their "manifest destiny," a collision of cultures became the advancing shadow of Black Hawk's life. By most accounts proud and belligerent, he and his band of dissidents clashed with the settlers and military forces sent to protect them.

In 1825 a treaty including many tribes in the region was executed, at Prairie du Chien in Wisconsin; the chiefs hoped to mollify younger, more militant men by drawing intertribal boundaries that would keep the fur trade open and, theoretically, all parties at peace. Two years later Black Hawk began drawing his forces together to attack Sioux braves who had encamped in an area along the De-Moines River that had been part of the Sauks' old domain. It took a combined effort by Sauk and Fox chiefs to persuade Black Hawk not to make war.

Arrested in 1828 for attacking keelboats, Black Hawk was imprisoned but soon released for lack of evidence. The westward march of white yeoman families and miners forced him to cope with a power structure he saw as dominating and regulating his people.

With the Indian Removal Act of 1830, Congress and President Jackson had a strategy: to buy up native lands and step up the pressure, pushing Indian nations farther west, thus providing land for the march of frontiersmen. Yet the dynamics of dealing with chiefs over boundary conflicts, trading issues and treaty propositions lay in the hands of federal Indian agents, men who had to deal with a range of subtleties. By 1830, the officials involved with Sauk, Fox and other tribes in southern Wisconsin and northern Illinois recognized problems with the Indian tradition of paying reparations to a community when someone had been wrongfully killed. As border disputes intensified, so did killing; the yearly sums the government paid to tribes and the Indian earnings from the fur trade were not enough to continue death-compensation payments. The government agents reasoned that if the United States agreed to cover payment for such settlements, turf wars among Indians would be reduced. Yet the agents also realized that the government had hardly honored its own obligations in the 1825 treaty. Thus the call went out for tribal leaders to attend another treaty conference, in Prairie du Chien.

A Fox contingent of sixteen men and one woman, en route to the conference, was attacked and most of its members killed by raiders from the Sioux and two other tribes. As the Sauk prepared to avenge their tribal allies and as the Sioux mounted for another attack, a government agent intervened and managed to revive the treaty council.

On July 15, 1830, the Sauk and Fox sold the remains of their country east of the Mississippi to the United States government. Black Hawk boycotted the ceremony and quarreled with Keokuk, the Sauk chief who approved the treaty. Black Hawk wanted to organize a militant resistance, linking Indians from Rock Island to Mexico in a fight against the Americans—a plan the chiefs' council did not embrace. Strife continued among various tribes; Black Hawk and others avenged the deaths of the Fox who were killed en route to the treaty with an attack on Sioux and Menominees that left twenty-eight of his enemies dead.

The government, meanwhile, had begun selling land on Rock Island in October of 1829, and by 1832 had sold some three thousand acres, most of it on Indian settlements. As whites moved into the area in growing numbers, alcohol production accelerated; whites cheated Indians out of their personal property, including guns. Indians broke through the fences white men had erected and smashed their whiskey barrels, even as the tribal council tried to effect peaceful relations with the federal government. The treaties had divided the Indians. The old fabric of Sauk life was eroding before Black Hawk's eyes; he himself was beaten by a group of whites.

The conflict came to a head in the spring of 1831, when Black Hawk and his men returned to the village from a long hunt that had not gone well, and found white settlers dividing up their ancestral land. The settlers had damaged their lodges and destroyed the corn crop planted by their women. Meeting with government agents, Black Hawk demanded that the white intruders get out. "I now determined to put a stop to it," he recounts, "and told them, that they must and should leave our country—and gave them until the middle of the next day."

Black Hawk's men repaired the lodges that the whites had damaged. Keokuk, the Sauk leader who had signed the fateful treaty, tried to negotiate a compromise but failed.

"There was no more friendship between us," reports Black Hawk. "I looked upon him as a coward."

And yet, with the sense of justice that pervades his memoir, Black Hawk allowed a white settler who had a large family to remain in the fertile village area if he "promised to behave well." In his rebellious stance, Black Hawk was now a leader to whom his holdout followers looked for survival.

In splitting off from the chiefs' council, Black Hawk's band of warriors had also isolated themselves from the regional Indian agent, their central link to the government. Part of the band was drawn from relatives of the Fox who had been murdered in 1830. In sum, the rebellious holdouts were a minority within their own culture. The chiefs were in the process of cutting their losses and moving on, taking the majority of Indians in the area.

As Black Hawk assessed his position, White Cloud, the so-called Winnebago Prophet, leader of a Winnebago community upstream on the Rock River, encouraged him to fight the Americans, insisting that Pottawatomies of Northeastern Illinois and Winnebagoes of the Rock River Valley would close ranks behind him. Black Hawk received word from White Cloud, who was believed to have spiritual powers and prescient dreams (hence, his status as the Prophet) that a "great war chief" was en route to Rock River with troops. This was Major General Edmund P. Gaines, a hero of the War of 1812 who had fought with Andrew Jackson's forces against the Creek and Seminole.

Black Hawk was now nearing sixty-five, and the Prophet, a generation younger, shared his passion to maintain Indian hegemony over the region. At a meeting with Black Hawk, the Prophet shared a dream: the white chief's intent was "to *frighten* us from our village, that the white people might get our land for *nothing!*" Reluctant to start a war, wanting only to preserve his land, Black Hawk's forces waited, nervously, as the federal troops took up stations across the Mississippi.

"Their village," wrote General Gaines, "is so situated that I could from the steam-boat destroy all their bark houses (the only kind of houses they have) in a few minutes, with all the force now with me, probably without the loss of a man. But I am resolved to abstain from firing a shot without some bloodshed, or some manifest attempt to shed blood, on the part of the Indians."

Black Hawk and his followers met with Gaines, and in the ensuing argument, the general told him, "My business is to remove you, peaceably if I can, but *forcibly* if I must!"

In his memoir, Black Hawk replies, "I never could consent to leave my village."

The Indians stressed that *they* had never signed an agreement to give up their land on Rock Island; they did not want war with the general—they wanted to stay where they had been living. Keokuk assured Gaines that some fifty families would follow him in leaving the area, and entreated the general not to use force against Black Hawk and his holdouts until the others left. Keokuk needed time to vacate, as the corn-planting season was nearly done and they wanted to harvest their crop before moving.

Again Black Hawk met with the Prophet, who told him to send the daughter of another chief to meet with the white chief and plead their case anew. Gaines rebuffed the woman. Rather than provoke a fight, Black Hawk's community went about their business as the war-boat passed menacingly close to their shores. When a mass of Illinois militia joined Gaines's troops, the Indians fled across the Mississippi and pitched camp below Rock Island.

On June 30, 1831, Black Hawk and others signed an agreement pledging that they would never return to the east side of the Mississippi without permission of the government. In return, Gaines promised that they would be provided corn to supplant that which they had left growing in the fields.

"The immediate aftermath of the affair," writes Wallace

was a torrent of verbiage, all white persons concerned in it being eager to justify their actions. Depositions, official reports, and copies of letters were accumulated by the dozen, for transmittal back to Washington, to show that Black Hawk's band was a savage military force which had invaded Illinois, attacked peaceful settlers, and was planning to drench the frontier with blood . . . The story of the deputation of Sauk and Fox Indians who had gone among the tribes of the Southwest and the relation of the Black Hawk band to the British and to the Winnebago, Potawatomi, and Kickapoo was touted as demonstrating an intention of the whole tribe to organize a general war against the United States, with military aid from Canada. Governor Reynolds was embarrassed when he discovered that the settlers were digging up the bones in the old Indian graveyard and burning the remains.

By winter of 1831 corn and food were in short supply. Facing starvation, Black Hawk and his followers returned to the now-forbidden Rock Island; he had about five hundred warriors and the same number of women and children. The group began moving north to meet the Prophet. The Winnebago leader assured them that a new white chief—General Henry Atkinson, who had replaced Gaines—would not attack so long as they acted peaceably.

Black Hawk's faith in the Prophet is a sad reflection on the eroding Indian hegemony in the region; for in fact the Winnebago were also divided—some supporting Black Hawk and others, north of the Wisconsin River, set against him—and the dreams proved hardly prophetic. As word spread of the returning Sauk families under Black Hawk, the governor of Illinois issued a call-to-arms and the United States Army sent more troops.

What came to be known as the Black Hawk War began in spring 1832 as a mistake. Atkinson sent messages to Black Hawk, ordering him off the land; Black Hawk sent word back that he was traveling north (away from his ancestral village) to the Prophet's land, there to make corn.

The Sauk-Fox braves were soon drawn into combat with a military force that outnumbered them two to one. Drunken guards in an advance party led by Major Isaiah Stillman killed three Indians, who had approached them peacefully, under a flag of peace, near Sycamore Creek on the night of May 14. Those deaths confirmed Black Hawk's suspicions about white motives, and he attacked.

Forty Indians routed Stillman's 270 soldiers, killing a dozen white men.

"The dead that were found were cut and mangled in a most indecent way; their hearts cut out, heads off, and every species of indignity practised upon their persons," a sentry wrote.

Fortified with arms and supplies from Stillman's troops, Black Hawk removed the Indian women and children to Lake Koshkonong, Wisconsin, and led his warriors back into Illinois. As word spread among settlers about Stillman's mutilated soldiers, a legend arose of Black Hawk as a fierce, cunning Indian of shrewd military prowess.

He was indeed a fierce combatant; but it was a rearguard battle all the way, fought more over food than freedom. An Indian sensibility—the idealizing of land as good and space as plentiful—was dying with each treaty that reduced their land. Neither a tragic nor a romantic figure, Black Hawk was at war with history's chessboard that sought to make of him a pawn.

Less than a month after Stillman's defeat, Black Hawk's men were beating their own retreat under fire from General Atkinson's forces, backed by reinforcements from the Illinois volunteer militia. Pushed back to Lake Koshkonong, where a batallion of lead-mine rangers from Wisconsin joined the U.S.-Illinois troops, the Indians scrambled up cliffs at Prairie du Sac on the southern side of the Wisconsin River.

"With consummate skill," wrote Reuben Thwaites, "Black Hawk made a stand at the summit of the heights, and with a small party of warriors held the whites in check until the noncombatants had crossed the broad river bottoms below and gained shelter upon the willow-grown shore opposite."

As the war dragged on that summer, newspaper reports rocked the establishment in Washington, prompting President Jackson to send Major General Winfield Scott, a hero of the War of 1812, into action; however, Scott's men were thwarted by a cholera outbreak.

Black Hawk tried to surrender, but his enemies wanted to eradicate Sauk rebelliousness. In a cruel irony, the whites found allies in Menominee and Sioux warriors who, in settling old scores with the Sauk, expanded the ledger of lost Indian lands. In a final indignity, a band of Winnebagoes—the same tribe of the Prophet, whose "dream" advice Black Hawk heeded—joined the hunt for Rock Island's last free Indians.

A third surrender was refused and in the end it was a rout, with three thousand whites stalking remnants of the one thousand men, women and children with whom Black Hawk had begun. Three hundred Indians, staving off hunger, their weapons lost, began crossing the Mississippi as the full weight of white anger rained down upon them. "They tried to give themselves up," states Black Hawk, "but [the whites] commenced *slaughtering* them! In a little while the whole army arrived . . . As many women as could, commenced swimming the Mississippi, with their children on their backs. A number of them were drowned, and some shot, before they could reach the opposite shore."

Most of those who did make it across, including the women and children, were later slaughtered by the Sioux. About 150 Sauk survived. Black Hawk escaped to a Winnebago camp, where they soon turned him over to the Americans. Prophet also surrendered, having failed to fortify his flanks.

The Black Hawk War had galvanized the white popular imagination through newspaper reports of bloody savages; yet as is often the case when a powerful country defeats a rebel force, the defeated warrior became an object of fascination. Whites who served in the various contingents would wear those experiences as accolades in later years: Abraham Lincoln served in the Illinois Mounted Volunteers, and another future president, Zachary Taylor, led troops and was garrison commander at Prairie du Chien. Volunteer horsemen included three future governors of Illinois—Thomas Ford, Joseph Duncan, and Thomas Carlin—as well as Colonel Henry Dodge, who would later become governor of Wisconsin.

A young lieutenant named Jefferson Davis, who later led the Confederacy, escorted Black Hawk, his two sons, the Prophet and a contingent of braves to prison. The captives were taken by steamboat down the Mississippi to a stockade near St. Louis.

"On our way down," Black Hawk tells us, "I surveyed the country that had cost us so much trouble, anxiety and blood, and that now caused me to be a prisoner of war. I reflected upon the ingratitude of the whites, when I saw their fine houses, rich harvests, and every thing desirable around them; and recollected that all this land had been ours, for which me and my people had never received a dollar, and that the whites were not satisfied until they took our village and our grave-yards from us, and removed us across the Mississippi."

General Atkinson, as victor, treated Black Hawk with a respect that competing warriors often accord one another—a sentiment that Black Hawk returned, in dedicating his autobiography to the general: "The path to glory is rough, and many gloomy hours obscure it. May the Great Spirit shed light on your's—and that you may never experience the humility that the power of the American government has reduced me to, is the wish of him, who, in his native forests, was once as proud and bold as yourself."

The words were written well after the winter he spent in prison at Jefferson Barracks, depressed at having to wear a ball and chain. He met the novelist Washington Irving, who described Black Hawk and his braves as "a forlorn crew . . . emaciated and dejected."

"Chief Keokuk interceded for them and pleaded for their release," writes Katharine C. Turner in *Red Men Calling on the Great*

White Father, an inspired history of Indians who visited presidents. After spending the winter in prison, Black Hawk, his two sons, the Prophet and two others were taken to Washington to meet with President Andrew Jackson, who followed a long-standing chief executive practice of trying to persuade defeated Indians that warfare was futile. Exposing Indian leaders to the seat of government, to museums and restaurants, to hotels and the spark of commerce, the presidents felt, would achieve more progressive results than taking tougher measures on the chiefs.

When Black Hawk's party reached Frederick, Maryland, he was struck by the sight of a "wonderful" road—"They call it a railroad . . . It is the most astonishing sight I ever saw. . . . I prefer riding horseback, however."

On April 23, 1833, the Indians entered the War Department, surrounded by a crowd that let out a cheer for them. Owing to his status as a chief, the Prophet went first, "tall and dignified," writes Turner. Her descriptions are drawn from accounts in the New York *American*. The Prophet had "debonair mustachios and a slight curl to his upper lip." Black Hawk was next, "a little man . . . remarkable for his 'pyramidal' forehead and hypnotic eyes. He reminded Philadelphians of Sir Walter Scott . . . and Virginians thought he resembled James Madison." Black Hawk's son and adopted son followed, along with the Prophet's brother and adopted son.

They were shown the portraits of Indians who had visited the White House: some had been their allies, others enemies of wars past. Then they were ushered into the office of President Jackson, the white-haired former general who "had seen as many winters as I had," Black Hawk would say in his memoir. Jackson, who had defeated the Creek in Florida and in Alabama, was sixty-five, the same age as Black Hawk.

Reminding them that they were hostages, Jackson said, "It is only necessary to deport yourselves peaceably and with propriety. Your detention is mainly dependent upon your good conduct." If they obeyed the treaty signed in 1832, they would have safe passage to their families and friends.

Although Black Hawk had been the battle leader, the Prophet was ranking chief, and so he rose first, wearing moccasins and pantaloons of tanned leather, with a scarlet mackinaw blanket across his shoulder. He invoked "the Great Spirit of myself and forefathers to witness the purity of my heart on this occasion . . . discovering that war had been waged against my tribe, I could not return to that tribe in peace; the consequences I now regret." Pledging his sincerity, the Prophet proffered a peace pipe, which President Jackson and his advisors took turns puffing. The Prophet closed with a request that they be allowed to return to their people.

The moment shifted to Black Hawk. He too wore a red blanket as he stood and met the president's gaze. "I am a man and you are another," said Black Hawk.

According to the New York *American* he then said, "We did not expect to conquer the whites. They had too many houses and too many men. I took up the hatchet, for my part, to revenge injuries which my people could no longer endure."

"Keokuk once was here," he said, referring to the Sauk chief who had capitulated in the treaty-making process. "You took him by the hand, and when he wished to return to his home, you were willing. Black Hawk expects that, like Keokuk, we shall be permitted to return too."

"You are too old not to do good," the president rejoined, "and on your return to your nation you can instruct the young men how necessary it is to preserve the peace . . ."

Although Black Hawk's autobiography does not acknowledge it, the White House meeting ended his strategy of rebellion. Now that he was old and no longer able to fight, the best he could expect was to get back to his people and adjust his horizons accordingly.

Presenting a peace pipe of his own, he beseeched the president for food and protection for Sauk women and children. Jackson assured the group that "those circumstances would be duly weighed" with orders to protect women and children, again premised on the Indians' behavior.

Katharine C. Turner picks up the story: "The President is said, then to have presented Black Hawk with a sword and medal together with some clothing, which he was to distribute among the other members of the delegation. Among these clothes may have been the military suit, complete with hat, gold epaulets, and brass buttons in which Black Hawk was buried five years later."

With a cordial round of handshakes, the Indians left.

They spent the next six weeks at Fortress Monroe near Old Point Comfort, Virginia, where they were treated well, yet had to bide their time before returning—a sign of the government's power over their movements. Black Hawk sat for an artist who painted his portrait; several more would be done in the weeks to come on his return trip, which proved to be disastrous for the president.

At Norfolk they toured the naval harbor where Black Hawk was delighted to find that the vessel *Delaware* had an Indian warrior carved upon its prow. He stood on the balcony of his hotel with the Prophet before a large crowd. Like triumphant politicians, the defeated Indians waved and offered best wishes to the curious and enthusiastic people. On June 6 they went to Baltimore where Jackson was making a stump appearance of his own. Both men attended the theatre that night, and Black Hawk was again well received. They were together the next day when Jackson's speech was that of a victor, reminding the red men of the futility of "raising the tomahawk against the white people, and killing men, women and children upon the frontier . . . Your chiefs have pledged themselves for your conduct, and I have given directions that you should be taken to your country."

From Baltimore the Indians traveled to Philadelphia, marveling at the prosperity and prowess of the cities. But the glowing press accounts of Black Hawk's journey apparently got under Jackson's skin. He did not attend a scheduled theatre performance; Black Hawk did. A newspaper speculated that the president must have felt "utter contempt . . . for the senseless crowd." Jackson pushed on to New York, riding horseback in a parade down Broadway where, the New York *American* observed, "the only disappointment in the assembled multitude seemed to be, that Black Hawk and his friends did not form part of the cortege."

On June 4 both men were scheduled to attend the takeoff of a hot air balloon; Jackson did not show. As the balloon rose, Black Hawk marveled, "I think he can go to the heavens, to the Great Spirit." Jackson's absence said a lot. "He would not again be seen in the same lion cage with the little old red man," writes Turner. In New York Black Hawk was a celebrity—the noble savage—and crowds were so tight in front of his hotel that his party was rerouted to another. Ladies were reported to have kissed him, and a gentleman gave him a pair of topaz earrings, set in gold, for his wife. He took in a fireworks display and had another night at the theatre; he greeted adoring throngs from the second-story window of his hotel, dressed in a frock coat, waving his top hat.

Black Hawk "was making a monkey" of the president, writes Turner. "The triumphal tour had turned into a farce. How the Indian must be laughing behind that stolid mask."

But the sweet irony did not leave Black Hawk haughty. In dictating his memoir later that year, he made no denigrating reference to Andrew Jackson. He could hardly afford to.

The Indians began the final leg home. A London publisher who boarded a steamer in Buffalo traveling through the Great Lakes would write of Black Hawk that he was "dressed in a short blue frock coat, white hat and red leggins tied around below the knee with garters . . . His shirt not very clean . . . His nose perforated very wide between the nostrils, so as to give it the appearance of the upper and under mandibles of a hawk. He wears light colored leather gloves, and a walking stick with a tassel."

The Indians posed for portrait artists, whose renditions would become collectors' items. Crowds gawked as the Indians went to theatres and restaurants, but when they arrived by boat in Albany, with a huge crowd lining the dock, ugly epithets rose out of the throng, drawing the curtain on the goodwill tour.

Black Hawk sat for another portrait in Detroit. The fascination demonstrated by easterners gave way to expressions of smoldering resentment in the heartland. At Detroit they were burned in effigy. They crossed Lake Huron to Mackinac and then Green Bay, and from there went in an open boat along the Fox and Wisconsin rivers, eventually reaching the Mississippi.

A ceremony was held when they returned to Rock Island. Keokuk, the chief who had accepted compromise for peace, arrived to greet Black Hawk. When Major John Garland read a document directing the vanquished Black Hawk and the Prophet to "follow Keokuck's advice and be governed by his counsel in all things," Black Hawk uttered a protest. Garland apparently did not understand what he said. Donald Jackson quotes from a letter by the major to the Secretary of War: "The old man rose to speak, but was so much agitated and embarrassed that he said but few words, expressive of dissatisfaction, and sat down. He, however, soon discovered that he had gone too far, and begged, that what he had said might be forgotten."

Black Hawk settled in a rural Wisconsin community near the

Iowa River with his wife, two sons and daughter. It was there that he dictated his autobiography to Antoine LeClaire, a government interpreter of mixed Indian ancestry. Jackson writes that Black Hawk was friendly to the white families who lived in cabins near his own.

The book gave Black Hawk more than a niche in history; it provided a persona, proud and resilient, showing his very life to be an act of resistance against the rapacious frontier culture that has since become mythologized by the machinery of Hollywood, with Indian-fighting cowboys like John Wayne made over as iconographic great men. The historical truth is much different.

In *Southern Travels*, an 1834 journal written by John H. B. Latrobe, who traveled down the Mississippi to New Orleans, the November 29 entry reads:

> One of our passengers last evening told me that about a month since he was at St. Louis, and went to pass an hour on board the "Museum Boat"—a floating collection of curiosities. Here, who should he find but Black Hawk the Prophet and some young Sacs, forming a part of the show and hired to be in attendance. Towards the end of the evening, Black Hawk addressed the company through an interpreter, informing them, that he was now very poor and without any money, and that if they would make up a collection for him one of his young men should dance the war dance for them. This was agreed to, the dance was danced and a collection of $10 to $15 made on the spot. How pitiable—how melancholy— the red warrior who but a few brief months ago was at the head of a brave band of his countrymen & friends, endeavouring to wage

war against the white man, their invader and their curse, is now turning his warriors into buffoons to win a melancholy one—but what help there is for it. Civilization will pass on among them and they must be trampled beneath its footsteps or flee where they cannot follow them.

Latrobe's diary does not have a comma between Black Hawk and "the Prophet"—but the inference is clear: his old ally was still on the road with him, this time as fellow entertainer.

The pathos that an educated white man felt on hearing of Black Hawk so reduced in circumstances conveys a sense of heightened respect associated with Black Hawk. Once a bloody savage, he was now in the estimation of a man like John Latrobe a symbol of nobility and courage.

Little is known of the Indian's final years. Could survival needs have reduced him to historical burlesque—wearing his medals, begging for coins? Or had the adulation he encountered in his tour of the East, coupled with the public's interest in the Indians, especially in his book, induced him to recast himself dramatically, tapping the legend of his own life, cashing in, as it were, as so many soldiers before and since have done?

My guess is that he created a small self-drama. Regardless, the *image* of Black Hawk, his hold on the imagination of the time, had by 1834 reached the point where he could attract money and interest from white people who just two years earlier had recoiled from grisly accounts of the Black Hawk War. His rehabilitation as a public figure is striking.

Latrobe's final line—that Black Hawk would "be trampled beneath [civilization's] footsteps or flee where they cannot follow him" is both prophetic and ironic. For Black Hawk's spirit did flee advancing civilization—and then surfaced slowly, deep in Louisiana, through the prism of a syncretistic religion that took his rebellion to its heart and soul.

There is no evidence that Black Hawk became a Christian. He eluded a missionary who tried to proselytize in the area where he was relocated; the missionary found Keokuk, who was impatient with his overtures. As the tribes went deeper into debt they had to sell off more of their remaining land. In 1838 Black Hawk and his family moved again, this time to a site on the Des Moines River. At an Independence Day celebration in Fort Madison where he was honored, the aging chief said bitterly: "I was once a great warrior. I am now poor. Keokuk has been the cause of my present situation."

He died later that year; his grave was robbed. "The governor of the recently created Iowa Territory obtained Black Hawk's skeleton and kept it on view in his office," writes Dee Brown in *Bury My Heart at Wounded Knee*.

The bones ended up in a museum in Burlington, Iowa. In 1855 Indians burned the building to the ground. And so there is no Black Hawk grave. But in Rock Island stands a statue commemorating him, which members of the Spiritual churches of New Orleans have traveled long distances to see.

The funeral of Black Hawk, painting by George Catlin; courtesy of
the National Gallery of Art, Washington D.C.

THE WORLD

OF LEAFY ANDERSON

Mother Leafy Anderson, founder of the New Orleans Spiritual churches; photograph by Michael P. Smith, 1974, of original photograph (probably taken in 1926)

I magine Leafy Anderson, catalyst of the Spiritual movement, as she posed in the 1920s for the photograph treasured by those who honor her today.

With fair brown skin and high cheekbones, wearing a pale gown and an Indian necklace, she is crowned with a tiara rising along lines of dark hair drawn tightly down the temples. At five-foot-five, she weighs about 190 pounds. Her mouth, with its strong lower lip, is a line of resolve. The contentment registers in her right eye, with its clear dark depth; the left one is blurred, but this is a photograph of a photograph taken from a distance of fifteen feet. The face conveys the affirming self of one who has traveled far to find a regal aura.

In late 1918, at age thirty-one, she left Chicago for New Orleans. Not much is known about her husband or why she moved her ministry to New Orleans.

What does "ministry" mean here? She begins holding services out of a small house on Melpomene Street, in central city, a neighborhood now overshadowed by a housing project. She soon arranges to rent space about two miles away in the Longshoremen's Hall on

Jackson Avenue, just down from the Mississippi wharves, and begins drawing crowds of five hundred people, including many whites, to her services on Sunday, Monday and Thursday nights.

Key material on Mother Anderson comes from interviews done in the Depression by the Federal Writers Project. The field reporters tried to capture folk dialect without the benefit of tape recording. "It was dere [in the Longshoremen's Hall] dat people saw Mother Anderson do some great work," said Mother Dora Tyson, one of her disciples, in an interview with Robert McKinney (himself a black) in 1939, nineteen years later and twelve years after Mother Anderson's death.

In the Longshoremen's Hall, explained Mother Dora, "she had to work cause ya know how dese people in New Orleans is. Dey think everything is fake. Well, Mother Anderson made 'em think different; she started to curing de sick an telling de darkies what was what an dey soon opened dere eyes an started follerin' Mother, yes, sir . . . Dat woman used to take in so much money she didn't know what to do wid it. Ise seen her wid so much as five hundred dollars on a Sunday morning. She believed in charging; she said de spirits couldn't wurk fo nothin' an dat she didn't fool wid dat kin' of spirits. Her spirits was expensive spirits."

She wore a robe of yellow and gold, overdraped with a mantelet bearing the image of Black Hawk, and three bracelets on her left arm that tended to slide off when she lit the furnaces on cold nights before services. She had a diamond ring said to be worth $250, no small sum back then, and on the street she was given to "loud dresses and fancy made shoes."

On Friday nights she held classes downtown at a place called Cooperative Hall, charging a dollar per person, with approximately eighty people per night. "She taught her students how to 'prophesy', heal, pray and see spirits," wrote McKinney, registering his skepticism about such prophesy with quotation marks. "They were instructed in how to read the Bible occasionally," he notes, the word "occasionally" hanging like a smirk.

Of the ten reverends listed as her leading students, two were white. From this group emerged several dynamic figures who created Spiritual churches in large buildings and storefront chapels as the belief system took hold during the Depression years.

In 1920 Mother Anderson purchased a three-story clapboard building at 2719 Amelia Street, a mile or so uptown, still in central city, a neighborhood pocked with poverty. The entrance door with its circular arch was framed by a pair of windows with ovoid-shaped arches. The fenced rooftop, where she arranged potted flowers, gave a vista of Magnolia and Amelia streets with their peeling duplexes and shotgun cottages, and a constellation of lights spread out below.

Today the Amelia Street building is a Baptist church; the old roof has been replaced, the upstairs deck is gone.

The reach of Leafy's life clearly found its grasp when she moved into her new church. Picture her on the roof deck, gazing at the stars—how consoling, and how empowering, to one who had struggled as she had. She called it Eternal Life Christian Spiritualist

Church Number 12, signifying a branch of the church that had been her focus in Chicago in 1914 and for several years before she moved to the South.

In the early 1970s, another of her key protégées, Bishop Bessie Johnson, told photohistorian Michael P. Smith that "Leaf" Anderson was half Mohawk.

Mohawk ancestry is an attractive notion in light of the Black Hawk rituals she planted in the folkways of the Crescent City. But given the dearth of documentation about her life, deciding what to believe about Leafy Anderson carries implicit risks. In many ways she is an enigma, an actress on the stage of history who, retreating to the wings, eludes those seeking knowledge of her truest self. She died unexpectedly, leaving little family and few papers.

Was Leafy her birth name—or one she took in the process of creating herself? The maiden name on succession papers of her estate is Williams; yet even that name is questionable—and when she married is unclear. The power of her personality suggests that she remolded herself after a troubled marriage.

The career of Leafy Anderson is a folk drama, with the odyssey of her life pulling Black Hawk's spirit southward. In the tracks of her years, the Indian's memory inexorably overtakes that of the seed-carrier, Mother Anderson. The riddle of Leafy's life flickers through Black Hawk's spirit-story like a leitmotif, a shadow-figure of the mighty warrior, his feminine other, a woman of mystery.

" 'The Life of Mrs. Leafy Anderson—Mortal and Immortal,' in three parts—the Woman, the Medium and the Mother. The singing of Mrs.

A. Price Bennett captivated the audience," reads a brief account in the *Louisiana Weekly*, the city's oldest African-American paper. "The play opened with a night scene in Chicago, then the home life of Mrs. Anderson was shown, her call to spiritualism, and her works. Mrs. Anderson played the leading role."

In a religious culture dominated by male preachers, Leafy was more than a sermonizer: as playwright-within-the-play, she makes her life episodes into ritual theatre. This is a woman who hires jazz ensembles to perform at her services, a far cry from most of the Baptist and African Methodist Episcopal churches, which utilized organs, pianos, or a capella singing.

Her crowning moment came in 1926 at a convention where colleagues of the Eternal Life Christian Spiritualist Church from Illinois, Florida, Texas and elsewhere met at her church in New Orleans. The conference included the reenactment of a historical theme: "Reverend L. Anderson illustrated Thanksgiving, beginning from 1620 down through 1926, which was wonderfully shown through songs and lecture." What is Leafy's concept of Thanksgiving? Certainly not the school parable of holy pilgrims and peaceful Indians. Presenting Black Hawk as a spirit guide was an act of revisionist history, a symbolic statement of *justice*. How precisely she enacted this we cannot say. But at the conference we find the first printed reference to the Indian: "collection taken up by Black Hawk, $17.83"—before a ceremony in which four "spirit guides" are introduced by Rev. L. Anderson, the others being Father Jones, White Hawk, and the Virgin Mary.

In its way, this quartet probably expressed her idea of a cosmology of spirits. The mysterious Father Jones (a reputed mentor from her years in Chicago) and the Virgin Mary occupy polar extremes. The two Indians, one White, one Black, are like poles of a racial spectrum. There is no reference to Jesus, though an interpretation of the Virgin Mary would presumably include Him. But when Zora Neale Hurston, doing anthropological research, visited the church the year after Leafy's death, she found that her followers did not mention the name of Jesus. "Jesus as a man was not important—he was merely the earthly body of a nameless 'Spirit' by which name the deity is always addressed," wrote Hurston in *The Journal of American Folklore*.

Music was an elemental strand in the spirit world of Mother Anderson. "The organizer of the Eternal Light Spiritual Church had a red hot six piece swing band that played the hymns in jazz time and style," wrote Robert McKinney, using Spirit*ual*, dropping the "ist," as the churches by the late 1930s had done.

"Mother liked her music and swung it down when she preached," Mother Dora said. McKinney continues: "From all indications she made the church swing all the time; there was more shouting than anything else for spiritualist congregations like nothing else than a loud commanding voice and swing music to back it up. One of the better Negro cornet players tooted for Mother Anderson—Chris. Kelley [sic]."

Born in 1891 on Magnolia Plantation, downriver from New Orleans, Chris Kelly was a pupil of Professor James Brown Humphrey, who made the rounds of outlying rural areas, teaching blacks on plantations the rudiments of brass band jazz. Kelly joined the Eclipse Brass Band in 1916. By the 1920s he was leading his own band and was "considered the best cornet man in the city," according to *New Orleans Jazz: A Family Album* by Al Rose and Edmond Souchon.

McKinney's favorable reference to Chris Kelly contrasts sharply with his secondhand account of the church rites: "Mother Anderson opened her services with songs (hymns), reading of the scriptures, prayer and then reading. Her collections were last on the church program and she ended with the 'Phenomena', which is telling selected individuals about their future, a very definite racket to land a few bucks without any hesitancy."

The hymns Mother Anderson sang included "When the Saints Come Marching Home," an early version of the song Louis Armstrong made famous in the 1938 recording "When the Saints Go Marching In," which is now an anthem of street parades. Her other selections were "I Expect to Spend Eternity Singing Around the Throne" and "Jerusalem, My Happy Home." Her favorite song was "I Will Guide Thee," which became Mother Dora's favorite, with lyrics as provided by McKinney:

VERSE: I will guide thee
          When Jesus calls me
          Sing on glad souls
          Let the spirits lead thee
          Walk in the light

CHORUS: Sing on glad souls, sing on

Keep the music ringing day by day

Sing on glad souls, sing on

Let the song of joy be your employ

It will cheer you on your pilgrim way

Sing on glad souls, glad souls, sing on

Two months after the ELCS conference, Leafy Anderson hosted the lecture of a visiting white Spiritualist churchman from Lily Dale, New York. The *Louisiana Weekly* of January 22, 1927, made reference to a "spirit cantata" given by the Bienville Club of Eternal Life, Spiritualist Mission. Bienville was the founder of New Orleans, and the use of his name implied a situation parallel to Leafy Anderson's being founder of the church—clearly she did not suffer from lack of ego!

Her spirit cantata was entitled "A White Man's Sin and a Squaw's Revenge." The drama is "set on an Indian reservation in New York City." What a suggestion—that the Indians who sold Manhattan Island now live on a reservation there! What is the "sin"? The taking of Indian land seems too tame. My guess is that she was commenting about rape as a historical theme, through a dramatic allegory of some kind.

"The powerful Indian guide takes control of Mrs. Leafy Anderson, an Indian squaw." Other individuals played Indian Joe, a hunter, and a nun. The character of the nun is a fascinating enigma. Was the virginal religious sister about to be assaulted by the white hunter, after he killed Indian Joe, only to be thwarted by the Indian Squaw?

"First class music," the column noted. "Admission 25 c."

Clearly, Leafy's ceremonies were spirit-summonings—she performed in the spirit's voice. The skits she orchestrated might be considered radio plays before radio. Thematically, they challenged conventional logic of race, religion and gender. In her own way, Leafy Anderson was a rebellious spirit. Whereas Black Hawk battled vainly to withstand the crush of white dominance, Leafy scattered seeds of a belief system that invoked spirits to ward off forces of the conventional world.

A drama of Indian retribution would have been charged with meaning for black people of New Orleans in the 1920s.

"Going back two generations, many blacks talked about their Indian heritage or connections," says Tom Dent, 63, a poet and civil rights historian. "My parents never talked about Africa. It was a blank on the map as far as what they related, whereas what you're seeing with these Spiritual churches are African remnants, no doubt about it. In the late nineteenth century some leaders advocated blacks going to Liberia—that idea was in the air all the way up to Marcus Garvey [in the 1920s], until the Liberians told him, don't come. Listening to my grandmother talk, she never mentioned Africa. But Indian blood was always mentioned. My great-grandfather came from Oklahoma, where he married an Indian woman and moved to Texas. My mother, in her application to Oberlin College, in piano, mentioned that she was part Creek. There was a psychological blotting out of African heritage in the early twentieth century.

"This was part of the legacy of racism," continues Dent. "People down here had little knowledge of Black Hawk. You find a dramatic element when you can introduce a new character to represent what you want him to represent . . . And there was a lot to that. The Indians did fight back, though they lost, under extreme alienation and pressure, and that rebellion was incorporated into American mythology."

Mother Anderson's obituary in the December 15, 1927, *Louisiana Weekly* says she was born in 1887 in Balboa, Wisconsin—a town that does not seem ever to have existed in that state. The death certificate says the body went to Chicago for burial. Was the fictitious birthplace a mistake, or an effort to blot out something in her past?

Before her arrival, a present-day male bishop said in a service, Spiritual people "had their little churches. They was hiding them all in little rooms, and going through the back doors. And all this time no one wanted to step out bold, standing up for what we believe in . . . She wanted to make the world know what God was doing for her."

Shards of biographical information on Leafy come from Bishop Edmonia Caldwell, a descendant of the Anderson family into which Leafy married. Born in 1924, Edmonia Caldwell learned of Mother Anderson through an uncle who had known her well. One of nine children who entered the Spiritual religion under Mother Catherine Seals, Edmonia Caldwell was entrusted with the family Bible in which Leafy recorded dates and key events of church and family history. The Bible was lost in flood waters that engulfed the city when Hurricane Betsy ravaged New Orleans in 1965.

"She was born in Norfolk, Virginia," says Bishop Caldwell, "and she moved from there to Chicago. Then she came to Raceland, Louisiana, with her brother, Lewis Anderson . . . Her maiden name was Anderson, and she married an Anderson. Her husband [William] was from some place down the bayou"—near Raceland.

According to Edmonia Caldwell, Leafy was born out of wedlock in Norfolk, which may account for the discrepancy in her stated birth place. Regardless, in Raceland, a rural town some sixty miles south of the city, she "got all tangled up with this man . . . She had so many herbs and fruits growing around her home in Raceland that people thought the herbs were for voodoo stuff."

She had a son, George, by William Anderson; however, things did not go smoothly for the couple. "He didn't like the Spiritual denomination," says Bishop Caldwell. "They always said this was voodoo work and used to call her a witch . . . She and her husband broke up because of her Spiritual work."

It appears, then, that Leafy lived in Raceland for at least several years prior to 1914, when her name first appears in a Chicago city directory. Caldwell says that she went from Raceland back to Chicago. The *Weekly* obituary identifies her as founder and president of the Eternal Life Christian Spiritualist Churches, "composed of twelve churches in various sections of the United States, the oldest being the [ELCC] in Chicago, which she founded in 1913. She was forty years of age, and had been preaching and healing for fourteen years. She is credited with several miraculous cures."

If her 1887 birthdate is correct, she was twenty-six when she founded the first church in Chicago—a young age for any minister, much less a woman recovering from a broken marriage, to launch a church. Black Hawk, says Edmonia Caldwell, "came to her in a vision in Chicago."

Could the obituary birthplace reference to Balboa have been a misspelling of Baraboo, a town less than ten miles from Prairie du Sac, one of the key battle sites of the Black Hawk War? Baraboo was also hometown of the Ringling Brothers circus. If she was born in Baraboo, then Black Hawk would have been part of the lore of her childhood, with circus life providing added spectacle. Alternatively, if she was born in Norfolk, perhaps she had reason for telling people otherwise. Did she want to avoid any association with where she was born out of wedlock?

Recently, one bishop said that Leafy "walked from Virginia all the way to New Orleans . . . carrying, spreading the Word, being a missionary for the Lord."

The word she spread was no echoing tone of Christian witness. Leafy Anderson was a Spiritualist—one who believed in the power of human mediums to communicate with spirits of the dead. Nineteenth-century Spiritualism flourished in the Northeast and Midwest. New Orleans had a concentration of Spiritualists, especially among the Creoles of color. The original movement, largely white, sought to prove immortality of the soul through communication with spirits of the dead. Many of the mediums were women. Spiritualism was marked by "rebellion against death and rebellion against authority," writes historian Ann Braude. By affirming the emancipation of women, Spiritualism threatened the male status quo.

Christians associated the occult with Spiritualism, which drew scorn and fascination in the popular press. The idea of trances, spirit visitations and God's immanence in nature clashed with Christian worship, divinity, and patriarchy. By the 1920s, a strain of Spiritualism had branched into sectarian Christianity. Without a firm dogmatic base, Spiritualist churches, with white as well as black adherents, split into a maze of tributaries. Some borrowed from the Catholic cult of saints; others formed around dominating, messianic preachers.

Leafy Anderson's ritual drama about her life points to Chicago as the place where her vision came together. Did she read the Black Hawk book, attend seances, or encounter the Indian spirit from Father Jones? How Leafy and Black Hawk met, in any case, is not nearly as interesting as the question of why they hit it off so well.

"When Mother Anderson first came down heah, she told us dat she wanted us to pray to Black Hawk because he was a great saint for spiritualism only," related Mother Dora Tyson. "She called Black Hawk to a special counsel for us. Ah know cause ah saw him. Yeah, Mother Anderson pointed him out to us an said, 'Dat's ya saint, chillun. Go to him for anything ya want. He'll never disappoint ya.' Well, ah was de first one to go to him and ah'm telling you he didn't disappoint me. Yeah, we had a special night to honor and pay our respect's [*sic*]to Black Hawk.

"No, ah don't know where Mother Anderson got Black Hawk from. Ah think he came to her one time and said dat he was de first one to start spiritualism in this country *way before* de white man come here."

Mother Anderson also dedicated a special night of celebration to Father Jones, "the great guiding spirit who controlled the other spirits," wrote McKinney. "He appeared to Mother Anderson in full dress clothes one dark and dreary night and instructed her how to master all evil, promising to stick by her at all times, according to Mother Dora. She says that Father Jones must have been a Bishop because he was 'de head man.' "

The late Bessie S. Johnson, another member of the seminal group taught by Leafy Anderson, had become an archbishop when photo-historian Michael P. Smith interviewed her in the early 1970s for *Spirit World*, his study of the churches. She said that Mother Anderson had "worked under" a Father Jones in Chicago, intimating that Leafy had a Spiritualist mentor of her own. Bessie Johnson also spoke of the founder's concept of "spirit returning"—when those who have loved a person return in the spirit to give guidance. "It's like when you hear an inner voice telling you what to do," she said. "That's one of your spirit guides. You should listen . . . "

"Spirit guides can be adopted from the living world or the world beyond," writes Smith, and received "either through a medium or through prayer." This idea of interweaving zones, between the spirit

Bishop B. S. Johnson with photograph of Mother Leafy Anderson;
photograph by Michael P. Smith, 1974

world and earthly existence, is both profoundly African and a sign of how the founder's vision has evolved.

In the 1930s a line of reverend mothers emerged from Leafy's tutelage to found chapels, storefront tabernacles and, in the case of Mother Catherine Seals, a semirural compound. Embracing saints and Christian witness, these women owed much to her.

"It was Leaf Anderson that told me I was gifted, and that I was born under John the Revelator, a beautiful guide and teacher," Johnson continued. "I preach through him. He's the one that saw Jesus as being the one who would loose the seals, and open up the Book of Life that we might have a right to eternal life."

Smith writes:

> Archbishop Johnson was born in 1893 in Baton Rouge, Louisiana, and grew up in New Orleans. Her mother was a cook. She doesn't remember her father; he died when she was very young. She was sickly as a child *and tells of being healed of blindness at age ten by a Sanctified man* [italics added]: "I was baptised with the gifts of the Holy Ghost at ten years old, and the Lord used me to his glory . . .
>
> "Every medium doesn't prophesy. I was given the gift of prophecy in Biloxi, Mississippi. I was by a [water] hydrant, and I heard a voice. That night we had a meeting in Biloxi. When I went into the grounds I began to prophesy to a lumberman that his daughter was going to walk again. And she did walk. She had not walked before that. Then I became a divine worker underneath Leaf Anderson."

Prophecies, healing, the stuff of New Testament miracles lived in the minds of Mother Anderson and the small group, mostly black women, whom she taught. So poor and ill-educated that some mispronounced her first name, they scraped along society's lowest rungs. Using Mother Anderson as a touchstone, they remade themselves, becoming healers and preachers, invested with spiritual power in the eyes of their people.

By the time she died in 1930, Mother Catherine Seals was the most renowned. "We are living happy together with Virgin children in here with me an other Virgin Wemon," stated Mother Catherine to the follower who took down her will, which she signed with an X.

"She was always taking people in who had no place to go and no one to help them," a white lady who had attended services at the Temple of the Innocent Blood later told an FWP interviewer. "She always had girls who had babies, or were going to have babies, and had no place to go, or their husbands had left them. One day she showed me a baby that she had confined. No, Mother Catherine was not a midwife. She lived so far out it was hard to get a doctor to come on time. That was why she had to confine that girl. That had happened several times. Mother Catherine took care of the mother and baby until they were able to take care of themselves. There were no men who stayed at the place.

"I never saw any miraculous cures but heard people talk about them," she continued. "I was told about a little Italian girl who was unable to walk and Mother Catherine cured her. Her parents brought her to the shrine and Mother Catherine kept telling the child to walk

Mother Catherine Seals, circa 1929

The Temple of the Innocent Blood, compound of Mother Catherine Seals (at center, in dark cape); probably taken in 1929 or 1930, photographer unknown; courtesy of Hogan Jazz Archive, Tulane University

and she left her place and walked to Mother Catherine . . . The parents had taken the child to doctors and they couldn't cure her. They told me that the child continued to walk and the parents gave Mother Catherine $500.00 for the cure . . . Plenty of white people attended the services and several studied under Mother Catherine and said that the classes were splendid."

Another reverend mother of the 1930s, Kate Francis, had a storefront chapel and a cult following. In an FWP interview after Mother Kate's death, her would-be successor said: "Her profession was a wash-woman. She made days like everybody else, just a plain woman . . . I don't reckon she made more'n one dollar and fifty cents a day. Mother was a country woman, you know. She wasn't married then, but she was a Christian, going to Mother Anderson's church. Fact was, she was a co-worker. 'Cause Mother prayed so hard and was so faithful the Lawd looked down in that tub in the boiling sun and opened His mouth one day. He says, 'You Kate Wilson, I'm goin' to give you a blessin' you ain't going to never fo'git. A lessin' that's goin' to turn yo' soul over in yo' body . . . Mother Kate said, 'What does you mean, Lawd? Does you mean that I'm supposed to heal and bless?' The Lawd must er said 'Yeah' 'cause she did all that.

"Sho', Mother Kate went to Mother Anderson. They all did. Mother Anderson called her and told her that she knew Kate had had a talk wid the Lawd. Mother Kate who ain't said nothin', said, 'Well, ain't dat astonishin'?' That sho' was astonishin'. Mother Anderson was a' astonishin' woman. Told her, 'Kate I done looked through the things the Lawd was talkin' to you about. You don't have to go back to no washin' and ironin' no more, 'cause you is meant to be a preachin' woman and you may as well start now.' I'm tellin' you Mother Kate went on through Mother Anderson's school and got the stuff. When Mother Kate Francis was fully full of the spirit and strengthened, she told Mother Anderson that she had got it, and Mother Anderson called on her to give proof. Mother Francis ain't done nothin' but told one of Mother Anderson's co-workers to lay down. The woman laid down and Mother Kate Francis ain't done nothing but pulled a live devil out of her stomach. This is sumpin' that ain't never been told befo', till now. They kept it a secret, 'cause she didn't want nobody to get scared."

Supernatural tales thread through various kinds of folklore. Mother Kate's alleged exorcism added drama to the revelations of the woman at the small tabernacle on St. Anthony Street, "known to many as 'Affectionate' but her name is Ellen Fairwell," wrote the FWP writer in November 1939. " 'I don't know what they is goin' to call me, cause I ain't been crowned yet,' Ellen stated, explaining that a crown of roses must be placed upon her head by thirteen of Mother Kate's co-workers and Father Louis Francis, Kate's husband, before she can truly call herself 'Mother Ellen Fairwell.' "

"Leafy Anderson often said that White Hawk was for the North and Black Hawk was the saint for the South," says anthropologist Claude Jacobs, coauthor of *The Spiritual Churches of New Orleans.* "There's obvious color symbolism in all of that"—meaning Black Hawk for blacks. "Spiritualism was tied up with Indian spirits throughout the 19th century. Her being a Spiritualist means that she's going to have connections with Indian spirits. They went hand in hand. If she's from the upper midwest, she would have known that mythology, heard those stories. . . . There was even some guy in the countryside around Vicksburg who was into banditry and had taken [Black Hawk] as his name."

At the end of his autobiography, Black Hawk offers his only known statement about black people, and in view of his spiritual standing today it might seem ironic:

> During my travels, my opinions were asked on different subjects—but for want of a good interpreter, were very seldom given. . . . The subject of colonizing the *negroes* was introduced, and my opinion asked, as to the best method of getting clear of these people. I have since made many inquiries on the subject—and find that a number of states admit no slaves, whilst the balance hold these negroes as slaves, and are anxious, but do not know, how to get clear of them. I will now give my plan, which, when understood, I hope will be adopted.
>
> Let the free states remove all the *male* negroes within their limits, to the slave states—then let our Great Father [the President] buy all the *female* negroes in the slave states, between the ages of twelve and twenty, and sell them to people of the free states, for a term of years—say those under fifteen, until they are twenty-one—and those of, and over fifteen, for five years—and continue to buy all the females in slave states as soon as they arrive at the age of twelve, and take them to the free states, and dispose of them in the same way as the first—and it will not be

long before the country is clear of the *black skins*, about which, I am told, they have been talking, for a long time; and for which they have expended a large amount of money.

I have no doubt but our Great Father would willingly do his part in accomplishing this object for his children—as he could not lose much by it, and would make them all happy. If the free states did not want them all for servants, we would take the balance in our nation, to help our women make corn!

This impractical scheme was not as bizarre as it may seem. Black Hawk stresses that he *was asked* about "colonizing the negroes" and how to "get clear" of them. His answer, says anthropologist Nancy Oestreich Lurie, an authority on Indians of the region, shows that "he is behaving in a very Indian fashion. He was faced with a question he knew little about, and didn't trust his interpreter. After thinking about it, the problem posed to him was that these people were not wanted, and his suggestion was to somehow absorb them. It seems racist on the surface but when you look closely it's not at all. There's a whole history of Indians adopting captives to make up for losses in warfare. He's not eliminating the possibility of their marrying into other groups."

Black Hawk knew little about slavery as practiced in the South; Indian captives might be held hostage for purposes of war, or assimilated into the culture of the new tribe. "He doesn't understand about Africa or colonizing people," continues Lurie. "He doesn't question if it's right or wrong, he's simply asked, what would you do? He's just being a good Sauk, thinking, if you don't want these folks, how do we absorb them?"

Such an absorption process had been going on in Louisiana for more than a century when Black Hawk dictated his remark. These links fired the imagination of black people and set the stage for Black Hawk's arrival in New Orleans.

By grafting worldly-wise jazz rhythms and ritual theatre onto a rock of Christian belief, Leafy Anderson made the Indian spirit *come alive* in an idea of faith as a memory of spirits. In so doing, she was translating a psychological language that, as Tom Dent contends, had been all but "blotted out" by racism.

Founded in 1718 by the Canadian explorer Jean-Baptiste Le Moyne, sieur de Bienville, New Orleans was a lackluster outpost of the French crown. Hard rains and heavy heat made muck of the streets, and mosquitoes festered in a climate as depleting as the politics. With two plantations and fifty slaves, Bienville enriched himself by selling slaves on the side, offering two Indians for one African to planters in the West Indies.

The roster of French emigrés who arrived in New Orleans in 1719 included prostitutes, thieves, a man accused of fifteen murders, and women who had led a rebellion in the Saltpetrie prison in Paris. Being sent to Louisiana was another form of punishment. "A special police force received a head tax for each person apprehended for possible deportation," writes Gwendolyn Midlo Hall in *Africans in*

Colonial Louisiana. "Members of the police force roamed around Paris and the provinces grabbing people for profit, their actions often based upon false accusation."

Survival in these latitudes was a struggle against hunger. The soil was not hearty enough for raising beef; the brutal heat and rains were not conducive to the growing of wheat or grapes for wine or many staples of cultivation that Europeans knew. Slaves toiled on plantations where indigo, tobacco, and rice were planted. Corn that the Indians grew was crucial to the common diet.

Townships began in certain of the Indian villages, but the crops and available game could not sustain the added human weight. Indian slaves killed settlers' cattle and used it for food. As African slaves began arriving in the 1720s, runaway blacks sometimes lived in Indian communities. "Because most African slaves brought to Louisiana were males, great numbers married Indian women, whom the French colonials had early enslaved as food growers, cooks, bedfellows, and translators," writes historian Jerah Johnson.

The sexual hodgepodge outraged the garrison chaplain. The priest fired off letters to Paris attacking Bienville, whose regime was barely able to feed or clothe its own soldiers.

The French shipped slaves from West Africa to Louisiana from 1718 to 1731. In the first four years, ten ships landed with 2083 slaves; however, many died along the way. Between 1726 and 1731, reports Hall, 4098 slaves boarded the ships and 3453 were alive when they reached Louisiana. Most of these slaves came from Senegambia, the region now encompassed by Senegal, southern Mali and

Guinea. Of these slaves the Bambara, as the French called them, were the dominant culture, an agrarian people from Mali who had resisted Islam, maintaining an animist religion that endowed spiritual forces in rain, earth, animals and rhythms of nature.

The Bambara also believed in a form of reincarnation or, as Hall writes, "transmigration of souls [as] a powerful source of cultural continuity . . . One person [in a family] replaces another, and the same spiritual forces are reused indefinitely. Life is transmitted intact."

Uprooted from a mother culture steeped in rituals of spirit worship, the Bambara and other Africans enslaved in Louisiana, mostly men, had to forge a language of survival, a vocabulary of resistance—some way of preserving the womb of spirituality, shorn of kinship and formal religious ceremony.

The Indian nations living around New Orleans and regions of what is now Louisiana—the Choctaw, Chitimacha, Chickasaw, Houma, and Caddo among others—began an inexorable retrenchment under French muskets and swords. In the 1680s, by one estimate, some twenty-four thousand Indians lived in the bayou lands of the Gulf Coast. Diseases brought from Europe and war waged by the French took a devastating toll. By the second decade of the 1700s, only seven thousand were still there.

In a 1718 account of the interior (what is now Cajun country) when Bienville was overseeing the construction of New Orleans are these words from a survivor of the Chitimacha tribe: "The water was troubled and stained with blood, our women wept unceasingly, our children cried with fright, the game fled far from us, our houses were abandoned, and our fields uncultivated, we all have empty bellies and our bones are invisible."

Indian nations shared compatible belief systems of a sort with the Bambara and other Africans. The woods and bayous contained spirit-forces that could change into human beings.

"The dead were respected and were dealt with carefully," note the authors of *The Historic Indian Tribes of Louisiana*.

If disturbed, they became ghosts—spirits without conscience or obligation. Ghosts were dangerous and greatly feared. Some living persons could talk with the dead and even ask them for favors, such as providing company or opening gates. Such conversations, however, were perilous and were available only to the most powerful persons.

Despite the Indian's belief that all events were part of a harmonic whole, death was traumatic, and the gaps left in family and community brought deep, genuine mourning. Although the dead were merely moving from one world to another, the path between the two might be an odyssey filled with dangers, temptations to go astray, monsters that might attack, or slippery logs that must be used to cross the streams. Consequently the dead were prepared for such eventualities. Food and water, favorite weapons, and sacred objects were interred with the dead to help with the journey into the next life.

Some tribes, among them the Tunica, made special fires to light the paths of the deceased. Others prayed at the graves and fired guns to frighten away demons and open the road.

These fundamental lessons for continuing life, provided by a religious imagination, were not unlike medieval Christianity's idea of death as a doorway that opened for the good soul's ascent to the embrace of God in heaven. As the saints served the faithful as intercessors with God, so Indians and Africans believed that their ancestors, if properly appeased, would guide them along the rocky road of life.

In the 1720s Spanish troops moved into northwest Louisiana, taking Indian slaves and establishing a fortress line against the French. In 1728 the French governor offered rewards to Indians for capturing African slaves, and forbade Frenchmen trading or living with Indians to keep black slaves. Some Indians did take slaves, Africans as well as other Indians.

As famine, disease and inner strife pulled at the social fabric of the Indians' lives, slaves fled whenever they could. In 1729 a group of fugitive Africans joined Natchez Indians in a bloody attack on French colonists 150 miles upriver on the Mississippi, killing 270 settlers, including women and children. The French, with help from Choctaw warriors and black slaves, recaptured Natchez and sold off four hundred Indians to the West Indies, with captured Africans sent to Mississippi slave camps whence they were resold.

The Africans who fought with the French were given freedom.

As the French gained the military upper hand, they stopped taking Indian slaves, in part because they needed their skills for basic sustenance. "The greatest misfortune which could befall the colony and which would inevitably lead to its total loss would be a union between the Indian nations and the black slaves, but happily there has always been a great aversion between them," wrote the French governor, Perier, who did not really know what he was talking about regarding a happy "aversion."

The French continued to foment trouble between Indians and Africans and between Indians and Indians; nevertheless, Indians were still harboring fugitive Africans into the 1730s and 1740s. Although we know comparatively little about their inner workings, these alliances would become a mythic touchstone in generations to come for blacks who felt a sense of solidarity with Indians. (This notion of a shared spiritual identity is problematic for present-day Indian leaders of Louisiana, many of whom reject it.)

By 1748, outcamps of Maroons—blacks and Indians—dotted the lower Mississippi, and in May of that year the governor ordered his troops to attack. Until that time, French fears of Indian attacks had overshadowed concerns of slave uprisings.

The colony was a drain on France. It did not produce the thick furs or array of spices and agricultural crops in such abundance as islands to the south. As the original melting pot of ex-convicts, prostitutes, backwoodsmen and soldiers bubbled along with heavy doses of imported rum, the French sent more respectable citizens to soften the harshness of its colonial brew.

Culturally, *La Nouvelle Orléans* was more an extension of the Caribbean than of the plantation societies of the upper South. As people of more bourgeois stock arrived, the seeds had already been sowed for a *culture métissage*, or mingling of bloodlines. The most remarkable products of this mixed-blood culture were the Creoles of color, descendants of African mothers and European fathers, a caste that by the early nineteenth century had a strong artisan class and its own aristocracy, some of whom owned slaves. Much less is known about African-Indian intermarriages, a bonafide Creole culture in itself, yet one whose pulse slowly sank beneath the flow of white, black and colored Creole peoples.

In the late eighteenth and early nineteenth centuries, as enslaved Africans of different ethnic backgrounds came to Louisiana from the upper South or the Caribbean, they were thrown together without a common mother tongue. Although the French required slaveowners to baptize slaves as Catholics, few went on to practice the faith.

A stronger force in the African psyche was the bedrock of spiritual memory. Creation myths might vary, but the sub-Saharan map was a blanket of animist belief.

To the Yoruba of Nigeria, life consists of interweaving zones: the living, the dead, the unborn. In rituals still performed, masked figures dance to percussive rhythms and invoke ancestral spirits, called *orishas*.

There are several variations of the Yoruba creation myth, in which a supreme being, Zeus-like, dispatches surrogate figures to found the kingdom. The dramatis personae, represented in masks and appeased in rituals, evince clear parallels with the gods and goddesses of the ancient Greeks. In each case, however, the *orishas* are acknowledged to have been actual people, whose memories live on spiritually, via the recall of a tribe.

"We can insist that the world of the unborn is older than the world of the ancestor," Wole Soyinka, the Noble laureate, has written, "in the same breath as we declare that the deities preceded humanity into the universe . . . and are an expression of its cyclic nature."

As early as the 1730s, slaves gathered at night to dance the *calinda*, a transplanted African dance set to hand drumming and some form of stringed instrument, a forerunner of the banjo. "Nothing is more to be dreaded than to see the Negroes assemble together on Sundays, since, under pretence of Calinda, or the dance, they sometimes get together to the number of three or four hundred, and make a kind of Sabbath," wrote a Louisiana planter in 1758. "It is always prudent to avoid; for it is in those tumultuous meetings that they . . . plot their rebellions."

A deep spiritualist sensibility channeled through those gatherings, a memory current that linked the slaves to the mother culture. "A characteristic of all African music," writes Francis Bebey, the novelist and musician from Cameroon, "is the fact that it is common property, a language that all members of any one group can understand."

In Africa the carved horns, gourds, calabashes, and sanzas surrounded the drumbeats and intensified the chants, with people enacting ritual drama through intricate dance steps or funeral processions in wide rings and long lines. They honored the dead for their existential presence, and they were not above comedic commentary on the deeds and misdeeds of kith and kin. In many tribes they wore elaborate costumes with masks—spirit faces of the ancestors or deities, of animals and nature forces.

In the "talking drums" of Yorubaland, as with the Ewe people of Ghana and drummers of other tribes, tonal currents of the drum communicated actual words. The drumvoice and the mask formed a continuum: the one gave words-as-tone, the other an imagery of spirit. Ritual memory—the center of gravity in religious worship—crossed the Atlantic in slaveholds of the Middle Passage.

Only now the masks lay buried in savannahs of the mind. Percussion in Louisiana—as on various islands of the Caribbean, as in Cuba and Brazil, all places where African slaves created spirit cults anchored to drumming rituals—had to be forged anew, in time away from the cruel logic of survival. Most runaway slaves brought before the Superior Council of Louisiana had fled plantations because of ill treatment or lack of food.

The social chaos that French governors beheld in those they ruled made for openings. Compared with the upper South's largely Protestant plantation societies, French-Catholic Louisiana was more lenient. In theory, master and slave were both Catholic. Freedmen of color worked as blacksmiths and artisans alongside slaves in the city. The *culture métissage* was more complex than any comparable society in the South. Although the government tried to suppress slave dancing in Louisiana in 1751, enforcement was weak. Where drumming was forcibly outlawed elsewhere in the South, in New Orleans it flourished.

Out of this environment emerged the North American city with the deepest African identity. It was shaped by what the historian Herbert Gutman called "cultural passageways," practices that Africans and their descendants forged to keep alive ritualized forms that bonded them to historical memory.

"Police regulations adopted during the French regime repeatedly castigated slaveholders for permitting slaves from several concessions to assemble for weddings or dancing the *calinda*," writes Carl Brasseaux.

> These gatherings were frequently held in New Orleans, where they provided a public menace because many inebriated participants "perpetuated a thousand thefts (*brigandages*)." Rural blacks relied upon their masters' working stock to transport them to nocturnal assemblies; in fact, the practice became so prevalent that in 1751, the colonial government authorized any settler to fire upon any of the "Negroes who work to death all of the colony's horses riding to excess."

Calinda dancing was one manifestation of African ritual memory. As subjugated people, Indians and Africans had to devise strategies for enduring and for keeping hold of core beliefs. As the number of Indians was depleted and remnants of the original tribes dispersed to outlying rural areas, any notion of actual rebellion tunnelled down into passageways of ritual memory.

In this respect the revolution on Saint Domingue had a profound impact. The slave revolt was launched in 1791 by a Voodoo high priest. When the island was liberated from the French in 1804 and renamed the Republic of Haiti, hundreds of French and mulatto planters fled, taking slaves with them. In 1809, some ten thousand people from Haiti reached Louisiana, by way of Cuba. Haiti had a much longer history than Louisiana of slave traffic with West Africa. Of the various Africans enslaved on the island, the Fon people of Dahomey (now Benin) were progenitors of a spiritual tradition with powerful properties. The Fon spirits were called *loa*, and like the *orishas* of the Yoruba people (who lived near the Fon in what is now western Nigeria) they were ancestral shades given supplication by the tribe. As the pioneering anthropologist Melville Herskovits reported, the most durable spiritual expression in Haiti was the *vodun* of the Fon-speaking people—"a word that is best translated as 'god,'" he wrote. *Vodun* has also been interpreted as "genius," or "protective spirit."

Dahomean religion centered on a hierarchy of *loa* whose human pasts lived on via recall of their descendants. The *loa* were not necessarily good or bad; their response to worshippers turned on the character of a given ceremony. Some two million Africans were sold into slavery by Dahomean kings; hence a powerful desire of slaves in Haiti was to appeal to the *loa* and *orishas* for help and protection.

Voodoo in Haiti resurrected Africa as a metaphysical impulse, a life-force for coping with a cruel and unforgiving world. What planter and priest saw as raw savagery—animal sacrifices, blood-as-symbol-of-life, dances with snakes—were expressions of a deep urge for rebellion that went through the ritual psyche, a reenactment of ceremonies rooted in cultural memory.

"Actually, *vodun* was Africa *reblended*," writes Robert Farris Thompson in *Flash of the Spirit*.

> The encounter of the classical religions of Kongo, Dahomey, and Yorubaland gave rise to a creole religion. . . . [with] a pantheon of gods and goddesses under one supreme Creator—deities who manifested themselves by possessing ("mounting") the bodies of their devotees. This aspect of *vodun* was reinforced by contact with French services for Roman Catholic saints who were said to work miracles. Chiefly from Kongo and Angola derived *vodun* beliefs in the transcendental moral powers of the dead and in the effectiveness of figurated charms for healing and righteous intimidation.

In the most famous melding of African deity and Christian saint, St. Peter, the first Pope, to whom Jesus gave keys to the kingdom—became Papa Legba, a Haitian descendant of a powerful African deity. In Yorubaland, the *orisha* is known as Eshu-Elegba (with alternate spellings, particularly Esu), while among the Fon of neighboring Dahomey he is called Legba. The Yoruba deity is a guardian of the crossroads between the living, the dead and the unborn. In both cultures Eshu, or Legba, plays a similar role as messenger of the gods. "Legba is the wild card of Fon metaphysics, the wandering signifier," writes Henry Louis Gates, Jr.

"Each god speaks a language of his or her own, and only Legba can interpret these," continues Gates. "For the Fon, Legba is a principle of fluidity, of uncertainty, of the indeterminacy even of one's inscribed fate"—that is, an ally with the potential to help the worshipper escape a seeming destiny. In certain spirit cults of Brazil, Yoruba slaves considered Eshu their liberator, an ally against the master class.

Eshu-Elegba is memorialized in wooden sculpture figures; he is often crowned with a hook coming back off his head like a curl. Variations of Eshu figures are amply documented in artworks from Nigeria to diaspora Cuba, where *santería* rites propitiate the *orishas* in spirit invocations of the drums.

"The tradition of guarding homes with images of Eshu came with black Hispanic people from the Caribbean to New York City and Miami in the decades after World War II," writes Robert Farris Thompson. "Today clay or concrete images for Elegba in the United States number in the hundreds."

The symbolic language of a culture arises from its core, a vocabulary encoded by sight and sound, rooted in historical memory. In music and dance, in costume and religious life, the past articulates its presence. Voodoo joined this language as waves of Haitians of Fon and Yoruba ancestry permeated New Orleans. The reach of African memory cradled a stretch of grassy plain behind the Vieux Carré along the ramparts of the town, girded by woods and swamp. Originally known as Place des Negres, then Congo Plains and later as Congo Square, it was a market where slaves mingled with freepeople of color and with Indians who lived outside the city. Indians played a ballgame called *raquette* in the area, part of which is now encompassed by Louis Armstrong Park.

The African-Creole culture had a profound impact on New Orleans. In 1782, as Louisiana shifted from French to Spanish rule, the governor barred the importation of slaves from Martinique, fearing a potential for rebellion in cults that "would make the lives of the citizens unsafe." In 1792 a similar decree prohibited slaves from Saint Domingue. By 1812 Afro-Caribbean culture had become a public spectacle at Congo Square.

The slave dances were now three generations removed from the first Africans who came to Louisiana. Yet even as the cosmology changed—the faces of African gods slowly turning into *vodun* visages of Christian saints—the ritual form endured: a large ring in which dancers summoned spirits to rhythms of the drums and strings, with cross-rhythms made by the dancers themselves. Here was a prototype of the ring shouts—tight human circles of call-and-response singing that reverberated in smaller gatherings behind plantation houses across the South. "The ring shout," writes Sterling Stuckey in *Slave Culture*, "was the main context in which Africans recognized values common to them—the values of ancestor worship and . . . of various other symbolic devices." Samuel A. Floyd, Jr., writes that the shout was a "holy dance":

> The participants stood in a ring and began to walk around it in a shuffle . . . These movements were usually accompanied by a spiritual, sung by lead singers, "based" by others in the group (proba-

bly with some kind of responsorial device and by hand-clapping
and knee-slapping). The "thud" of the basic rhythm was continu-
ous, without pause or hesitation. And the singing that took place
in the shout made use of interjections of various kinds, elisions,
blue-notes, and call-and-response devices . . .

The sustained impact of drumming at Congo Square was a spiritual force preserving a *form*, if not the literal language or purest
properties of African ceremony. By keeping these glimmers of memory aglow, the slaves gave light to their past.

In Dahomey, the rainbow serpent was a central deity, a resplendent coil of androgynous color symbolism: red for male, blue for
female. "Aggression and compassion are thus writ large across the
skies," explains Robert Farris Thompson. In one Dahomean myth,
the serpent erected four pillars "to hold aloft the sky. And then he
twisted around these columns in brilliant spirals of crimson, black
and white to keep the pillars upright. These were the colors of night
(black), day (white), dawn and twilight (red)."

Congo Square dancing was suppressed in 1835. The dance continued in woods, on bayous and at Lake Pontchartrain, with torch-lit
gatherings. In some of these cults, people danced with snakes,
snapped the heads off chickens and made blood sacrifices of goats.
The full range of these cults is unclear; but hard drinking and sexual
activity were reported in scattered "outside accounts" and several
interviews with elderly blacks years later.

How many neo-African cults cleaved to a purer spiritualism is unclear. In the passage across generations from Africa to Haiti and then New Orleans, any tradition as complex as *vodun* was bound to absorb shocks and reassemblings—how could it not? Under the harsh laws of mid-nineteenth-century Louisiana, where police sometimes stood outside of black Protestant churches to guard against political rebellion, it should come as no surprise that some of the people at the bottom of society who found their way to hybrid cults got liquored up and sexually explosive as drums pounded around fires lighting up the night. But how much of it was truly Voodoo, the syncretistic religion that fused with elements of Roman Catholic ritual in Haiti?

Voodoo is important to our understanding of the Spiritual churches. Africa reblended was one antecedent, one plank in the religious platform that Leafy Anderson built a century later.

Unfortunately, the chief reference, Robert Tallant's *Voodoo in New Orleans* (1946), is a highly problematic book. Tallant was a well-known New Orleans novelist and journalist. His historical writing was flawed by a racial paternalism, marring his analysis. Although his interviews with elderly blacks of the day are helpful, Tallant relied heavily on books and articles about Louisiana with scant research on Haiti or Africa; he had a near-tabloid obsession with sex and savagery. He also refers to Mother Dora Tyson as Mother Doris, an error which, while small, is troubling since the Dora Tyson WPA interview cited earlier is taken from the Robert Tallant Collection at the central New Orleans library. The interview was one of many by FWP field reporters to which he had access.

Nevertheless, Tallant amassed vital information on remnants of Voodoo, and, however skewed his interpretation, he provides valuable material on the two nineteenth-century priestesses both named Marie Laveau, women of color, mother and daughter, who wielded great influence.

The Laveaus, *mère et fille*, were precursors of a cultural role Leafy Anderson and the reverend mothers she trained would assume—woman as central figure of a worship tradition.

According to her 1819 marriage certificate, Marie Laveau had been born out of wedlock. "Newspaper reporters later wrote of her father as having been a wealthy white planter, of her mother as a mulatto with a strain of Indian," notes Tallant.

The man she married was a quadroon (one-fourth black) who had come from Haiti. Both were Roman Catholic. The marriage did not last long. She found a new partner by whom she reportedly had fifteen children. Tallant does not explain why she used her maiden name—a marked departure for those times. Working as a hairdresser, she became privy to the secrets of a European Creole society many of whose male members supported mulatto mistresses and out-of-wedlock children in shadow families.

Tallant writes: "Marie never lessened in any way the mysticism and sensuality of the fanatic Zombi worshippers—all the orthodox trappings of the spectacle were retained: the snake, the black cat, the roosters, the blood-drinking and the finale of fornication—but she added some new tricks, both borrowed and original, principally Roman Catholic statues of saints, prayers, incense and holy water.

The Voodoos had been devil-worshippers originally. Marie renounced this and always insisted that her people were Christians. She offered Voodoo to God."

Tallant got it backwards. By embracing the Christian rite, Marie Laveau was extending the syncretistic form so prevalent in Haiti: the icons and prayers and holy water were not "new tricks" but transplanted phenomena. The blood-drinking and "finale of fornication" were indeed new—if they occurred at ritual theatre presentations Marie Laveau actually staged, if it really was her, as hearsay accounts or those of white onlookers claim. The "orthodox trappings" were hybrid cloakings of an African religious belief system that in Haiti meshed one set of deities with Catholic saints.

However one labels those exotic activities, there is a reason why they were so popular. Neo-African spirit cults thrived in the French Caribbean, as they did in Cuba and Jamaica, in Brazil and other parts of Latin America. As the New Orleans dances lost the seminal quality of religious expression, the rhythm of rebellion rolled into a counterculture feast of the senses. The sheer outrageousness of it all probably drew some of the well-born young white women mentioned in the interviews and press accounts. Others reportedly sought guidance from cult priests and priestesses as people do of spiritualist mediums today. The semipublic Voodoo dances were spectacles in a city steeped in exotica.

Tallant writes that Marie Laveau "took charge of Congo Square," citing as his authority a ninety-five-year-old former slave's recollection of what he saw as a six-year-old. But no single person could have taken charge of an environment as spirit-charged as Congo Square. After Laveau's death, one of her daughters, Marie Glapion, born in 1827, assumed the name Laveau. Reportedly colder and harder in personality, Marie II carried on the tradition with help from one "Doctor Jim" (Alexander), a witch doctor. He was also known as "Indian Jim." Tallant writes:

> Doctor Jim was three-quarters Indian, one-quarter Negro, and he liked to pass as a Mexican. He had been practicing in the State of Mississippi for years before moving into the territory dominated by Marie Laveau, and when he came he brought with him much experience in the field, a reputation as a successful healer, and a white wife, who was a fairly well known Voodooienne herself. His powers of healing are said to have been remarkable.

He was renowned for his dancing at Voodoo-inspired ceremonies of the late nineteenth century—"a bizarre combination of the Calinda and an Indian war dance, performed in tights and with a candle balanced on his head," writes Tallant.

Showmanship was elemental in the imitated remnants of the Voodoo tradition—perhaps it was the catalyst that kept the hybrid gatherings throbbing along. More instructive for our purposes are the continuing references to Indians—in Marie Laveau's reputed bloodline, in Doctor Jim's, in the description of his dancing, and in the larger parallel between the ring shout and Indian ceremonial dances with their circular patterns.

More persuasive evidence of Voodoo's dynamic role in ritual

Altar at St. Lazarus Spiritual Church

Archbishop E. J. Johnson, pastor,
Israelite Universal Divine Spiritual Church

Black Hawk altar in the
home of Bishop Efzelda
Coleman and her hus-
band, Bishop Oliver
Coleman

Altar of St. Daniel Spiritual Church on Amelia Street

Black Hawk bust, Israelite Universal Divine Spiritual Church

Altar at Infant Jesus of Prague Spiritual Church

Walter Lastie on drums,
David Lastie on saxo-
phone, Betty Ann Lastie
on piano, in Guiding
Star Spiritual Church,
1979

"Black Hawk in the Bucket," St. Christopher Spiritual Church

Fruit Feast at Black Hawk celebration, December 9, 1994, Israelite
Universal Divine Spiritual Church

Big Chief Jolley (George Landry) of the Wild Tchoupitoulas,
in front of his house, dawn, Mardi Gras, 1979

Bishop Edmonia Caldwell

Betty Ann Lastie, piano, and Rev. Jules Anderson, in white robe,
tambourine, in Guiding Star Spiritual Church, 1979

thinking of the African-Creole culture is the language of the gods. A woman told Tallant that Marie Laveau "was real good to my aunt. She even taught her a Voodoo song. It went like this: 'St. Peter, St. Peter, open the door,/ I'm callin' you, come to me!/ St. Peter, St. Peter, open the door . . .' That's all I can remember. Marie Laveau used to call St. Peter somethin' like 'Laba.' "

St. Peter-as-Papa Legba is one spirit figure of a tradition that the Europeans could not entomb. The song to St. Peter could be transposed as a chant beseeching Eshu-Elegba, guardian of the crossroads, to admit the worshipper into the spirit world. In translation, a song to Legba in Haiti goes: "Papa Legba/ open the gate for me. . . . Open the gate for me, papa, so that I may enter the temple/ On my way back I shall thank you for this favor."

Against this background, the Black Hawk chant has powerful resonance. In the one I have heard, set to a rocking purr on the organ and the clash of palms and knuckles on tambourine, the faithful sing: "He'll fight your battles . . . he's on the wall . . . he's on the wall." While there is no evidence linking Black Hawk to St. Peter-Papa Legba in Leafy Anderson's designs, the Indian holds a comparable role as a prototype of cultural memory, a guardian "on the wall" between the church of the living and the world of the spirits.

Another mythic figure that emerged out of the spiritual tunnelling from Africa via Haiti to New Orleans was the serpent deity of Dahomey, known as Damballa-Wedo—first as the central figure of Voodoo worship, later as the snake image painted on the walls of Mother Catherine's compound when Zora Neale Hurston visited in

1928. In the 1970s Claude Jacobs and Andrew Kaslow, in their research of the churches, found

> an altar in the home of a minister whom we visited [that] held
> black saints and a plastic cobra in an upright position next to
> Jesus. When asked about this, the minister insistently denied that
> it was anything more than a piggy bank into which he put pennies
> for the saints.
>
> Aside from the possible incorporation of Damballa into the
> Spiritual churches' pantheon, only tantalizing fragments of evi-
> dence provide further direct connections with Voodoo . . . much of
> what has been accepted as descriptions of its rites were apparently
> performances, shows and celebrations held for public viewing or
> entertainment. Accounts of authentic or secret Voodoo worship in
> Louisiana are almost nonexistent.

The cultural memory that gave rise to Voodoo in Louisiana was
richer for the sum of its parts. The altars of syncretist religions
throughout the Caribbean form an enduring link with the Spiritual
churches of New Orleans. Glasses with water, flowers, fruit, and
wooden and plastic statues of the saints, interspersed with iconographic carvings of a given tribal type, place Black Hawk altars in a
constellation with the Indians of San Juan Chamula of the Yucatan
and with *vodun* altars of Haiti, to cite but two examples. These are
symbolic expressions of an inherited spiritual ancestry, whether African or Indian at root, like a series of bas-relief works that span the
Caribbean Basin, with New Orleans as the northernmost point.

Edward Kamau Brathwaite, a distinguished Caribbean poet and historian, writes of *kumina*, a Jamaican spiritual religion: "It is a situation, too, in which the god: spirit: ancestor: remains very close to the living: is in fact *part of the living*; and the 'worship' (the word is not even appropriate/ accurate here) involves the possession of the living by the dead: by ancestors; by the god; or rather, it involves the frequent and accepted incarnation of the spirit: god into the community of the living."

With Voodoo as one offshoot of African memory, the river of percussions pouring out of the ring dances spilled into diverse tributaries as generations of African-Americans moved beyond slavery. The currents branched into streams of jazz, rhythm-and-blues and gospel music.

Here a pregnant irony appears. The jazz idiom took its essential shape from the changes in brass band parades about the time of Reconstruction. Military cadences supplanted the hand percussions of African memory. Tribal drumming, such as it was, effectively disappeared. But the pulse of Congo Square flowed in the lives of street dancers who followed the parades. The scraping and thudding of feet on the street formed a cross-rhythm to the swishing of the snare and the thumps of the big bass drum. The body rhythms of parade dancers engulfing the bands were catalysts for the famous "second line"—the gyrating marchers whose body language beckoned a more sinuous, parade-time backbeat on the drums, fostering a dramatic shift away from the spine of military drumming in conventional brass band fare.

In second line music, the human architecture of the ring dances at Congo Square was rearranged—dancers in long sinuous lines opened the ring, stretching it out, coursing ahead, moving the African polyrhythmic sensibility on a more linear path of melody. The joy-shouts of parade people and the groundbeat of feet on the street surged with call-and-response patterns of the horns and woodwinds, playing off the rhythm and roll of drum syncopations.

A similar reassembling shaped the oral tradition of countless black churches, where cries of the faithful—"Yes, Lawd!" "Say it, now!"—answer the call of gospel sermonizing by preachers in the pulpit.

Second-line music was a seminal force in the birth of jazz, impregnating the emergent form with African dynamics. The music was anything but a folk idiom: many of the early jazzmen read sheet music, and a community of musical families among the Creoles of color facilitated the fusion of African polyrhythm with European instrumentation and melody. So too was there a large community of white ragtime and brass band musicians, especially among the Sicilians.

As the jazz idiom flowered, what happened to tribal drumming? Even if we accept the accounts on which Tallant relied to argue that a remnant of rhythms at Congo Square channeled into Voodoo-derived cult dances on the lakefront, the descriptions smack of a degenerate show.

As the second line supplanted the ring dances of Congo Square, going into the streets of New Orleans and thriving in the neighborhoods, clubs, parades and funerals, a new persona joined the procession of spirit figures—the Indian, as interpreted by men of African origin. The tribal percussion sensibility shifted to embrace the tambourine and handheld instruments, like bottles and sticks, played by black men wearing Indian costumes, parading through streets at Mardi Gras, singing a capella chants in rings outside and inside honky-tonk bars.

A formal linkage of black Indians with Mardi Gras began about 1883, nearly a half-century after Black Hawk's death, and four years before Leafy Anderson's birth. Carnival was the stage on which this new form of ritual theatre recovered an essence of African spirituality.

Carnival was a celebration of Christian origin that flourished throughout the Caribbean and parts of Latin America. At various turns in the nineteenth century, Indian costumes became an artistic motif in the carnivals of Trinidad, Haiti, Venezuela, Brazil and Peru. In some instances blacks dressed as Indians; in others, Indian peoples wore their own resplendent outfits.

In New Orleans, where the Anglo-European aristocracy created parade krewes steeped in the lore and imagery of ancient Greece, the masks and parades became a living theatre, a new threshold allowing the descendants of slaves to reassert themselves, this time as Indians. The full degree to which Indian bloodlines mark this tradition is still unclear, but the high cheekbones and distinctive facial features of some black Creoles are unmistakable.

By 1890 the word *griffon*, which meant "black Indian," had

been incorporated into the lexicon of the city's Black Code, a listing of racial types that was meant to preserve white purity and enforce the laws of segregation.

Strains of African-Indian intermarriage were an authentic Creole phenomenon, born in the New World yet dramatically different from the European-African miscegenation. One bond was wrought of two races thrown together by imperialism; the other from sexual domination of European men over black women.

Africans and Indians had hierarchical community structures, led by chiefs. Both groups honored ancestral spirits, both believed in spirits that occupied the natural world around them. As the white aristocracy emulated royalty with Rex, the king of Carnival, and with fancy balls where daughters of the elite were presented as princesses to courts of the carnival krewes, a black bourgeoisie tradition of balls and social clubs emulated the whites'.

Carnival-as-a-season filled a more profound void for poor blacks; it gave the descendants of slaves the chance to stage their own ritual interpretations of history. The Indian outfit—like the skeleton costumes with sinister skull masks that flourished alongside the Mardi Gras tribes—served as cover for an identity, rebellious or haunting, a body presence of freedom and revolt against the policeman, judge or Rex upon his high parading throne. Carnival provided the ritual stage for an extension of Congo Square.

In *Mardi Gras Indians,* Michael P. Smith trains the historical lens on the period between December 1884 and June 1885, when New Orleans was the site of the World's Industrial and Cotton Centennial Exposition. A large pavilion site was built on a section of what is now Audubon Park. The Buffalo Bill Wild West Show performed during this period, kicking things off with a huge parade with, according to a press account, "whooping red devils . . . Indians wore their semi-civilized garb, were gorgeous in their native war-paint . . . and went through the weird dances of their race."

Smith contends that the cultural form of blacks-as-Indians was a historical presence well before 1884, and that the Plains Indians costumes and performances at the Cotton Exposition had a galvaniz-ing effect on low-income blacks. My own reconstruction of the Mardi Gras Indian lineages for an earlier book discussed a Creole of color named Becate Batiste, a plasterer by trade, who formed a group of Indian masqueraders called the Creole Wild West. Whether that seminal Indian gang formed in 1883 (as a diary passage suggests) or during Mardi Gras of 1885, with the Cotton Exposition in full flow, is an academic point. The taproot of this Carnival hybrid lay in a mutual sense of rebellion between two oppressed peoples of Louisi-ana, each with a spiritual past.

More than mere celebration, the Mardi Gras Indians enacted a symbolic drama of the ritual psyche, an interpretation of the dreams of a common language.

The Mardi Gras Indian chants and tambourine rhythms were not a form of spirit worship per se; but through a slowly building body of verbal riffs and coded chants, they launched an oral history, prais-ing the Big Chiefs who lead the tribes, singing the equivalent of prayers, like "Indian Red," as the tribe sets out on Mardi Gras day, and laying down a body of lore that by the 1970s was shooting streams of chant-driven lyrics into pop music recordings like *The Wild Magnolias* (Polydor) and *The Wild Tchoupitoulas* (Island). The Tchoupitoulas tribe was led by one George Landry, a.k.a. Big Chief Jolley, an uncle of the Neville Brothers, who shaped the instrumental backing and sang wondrous harmonies on the record.

Nearly a century before Chief Jolley and other Indians began marching into record studios, the early Mardi Gras gangs resurrected a primal African essence in their ring shouts, with shuffling feet and human circles, moving to tambourine jangles out in the streets, with braves in radiant feathers and shimmering ostrich plumes. The braves surround the Big Chief as he calls out his tribe—the Spy Boy moves ahead, a messenger figure like Eshu, monitoring the terrain for movements of other tribes, followed by the Flag Boy, Trail Chief, and others down the line.

The Creole Wild West formed in the Seventh Ward, a downtown neighborhood; as part of the tribe moved uptown, a new gang emerged, the Yellow Pocahontas, in Batiste's neighborhood. A fascinating hierarchy unfolded as the folk tradition took shape in a loose constellation of tribes, or gangs, in low-income neighborhoods.

"When a Spy Boy would meet another Spy Boy from another tribe," Jelly Roll Morton told Alan Lomax, speaking of the early 1900s, "he'd point his finger to the ground and say, 'Bow-wow!' And if they wouldn't bow, the Spy Boy would use the Indian call, 'Woo-woo-woo-woo-woo,' and that was the calling of the tribes, and many a time in these Indian things, there would be a killing and the next day there would be someone in the morgue."

In *Up From the Cradle of Jazz*, I wrote:

> To mask Indian meant that the poorest man could transcend the toil of daily life, however ephemerally, in open defiance of the role society imposed on him. The tribes drew from laborers, dock workers, street hustlers, and common criminals, as well as from descendants of Indians and in later years from occasional musicians. Violence at the hands of whites provoked in some Indians a militant strain, suppressed through normal life, yet freed in Carnival. In the 1850s, Irish Channel whites openly terrorized blacks entering the area. By the 1920s, in the same neighborhood, whites dressed as cavemen fought the Indians with spike-studded cypress clubs.

More often, black Indians fought each other.

Allison "Tootie" Montana, a grand-nephew of Becate Batiste, has been Big Chief of the Yellow Pocahontas since the 1960s. In a 1982 interview, Montana told me about his youth and "men who'd walk the streets here, real dangerous peple. I'm talkin' about men who'd kill you with their fists. Stone killers. Today people run to the Indians. During them days, people would run away from the Indians."

"We were going uptown to a place called the Magnolia Bridge," Vincent Trepagnier said of his marches with the Yellow Pocahontas in the 1930s. "I don't know if you ever heard talk of it. It's torn down now. The two Spy Boys from the Pocahontas and the Wild Squatoolas got into a humbug over the bridge and shooting took place. . . . Well, that draw policemen, see?

"Now there was nowhere to go, so what we did, we jumped in the New Basin Canal with our clothes on. The policemen came and got some out, and some others they didn't. I stood right underneath the bridge till they left and then come on back home. I couldn't go up-town cause I was all wet."

Although street fights between Indians were tapering off by the 1950s, the violence of early conflicts bears scrutiny. They fought for the same reasons other poor people sometimes fight: out of anger and frustration, as an expression of masculinity otherwise subjugated, as a catharsis for the internal tensions of a community. The framework of Carnival gave heightened meaning to the costumes and fired a sense of rebellion, with ritualized battle sometimes spilling into literal violence.

"We used to fight with knives and guns," one brave put it. "Now we compete by the beauty of our costumes." The dazzling feathers, rhinestones and sequins in studded patches designed and sewn onto costumes over the months leading up to Mardi Gras are one of the most beautiful traditions of American folk art.

In the mid-eighties, after Big Chief Jolley died, one of his Wild Tchoupitoulas costumes was worn by the late James Anderson in Black Hawk ceremonies at the Infant Jesus of Prague Spiritual Church where his mother, Lydia Gilford, was bishop. She too is now deceased.

"If the Indians serve God, they're serving him in spirit. This is a spirit God," Bishop Gilford told folklorist Alan Govenar. "The Lord spoke to me one day and told me to get the small people together. He didn't tell me to get the big dignitaries. Get the small people and let the small people try to do what God wants them to do. I feel that if you have somebody that's trying to help you and bring your gift out, well, that's the one you want to be around . . . I started in my front room where I had to knock the wall down, and push it back. Finally, I had the whole five-room house the congregation built up. I did what God told me to do."

The use of Mardi Gras Indian costumes in the churches is rare. But some church members, including an occasional bishop, have been known to pop up at Indian practices—ring-shout dances with percussions—in clubs of the inner city. In like measure, some Mardi Gras Indians attend the churches.

When Leafy Anderson began her church in 1920, the black Indians of Mardi Gras had been at it for at least forty years. Leafy's appeal to the "small people" arose from her persona of empowerment. She remade a world marked by hardship and racism by holding out a world of spirits waiting to be summoned and appeased. As black men at Mardi Gras embraced the Indian persona and reconfigured the ring shouts, Leafy orchestrated a ritual drama with a more benevolent appeal to women. In Black Hawk she presented a protective masculine spirit, a guardian to be beseeched for a safe journey through the hard lives her people shared.

The roots of these churches lie in the years just after World

War I. As rural black folk migrated into cities, storefront churches and chapels began sprouting. "They want a church, first of all, in which they are known as people," wrote E. Franklin Frazier in *The Negro Church in America*. "In the large city church they lose their identity completely and, as many of the migrants from the rural South have said, neither the church members nor the pastor know them personally."

The large Baptist and African Methodist Episcopal congregations—or in New Orleans, the Roman Catholic parishes—guaranteed no sense of personal status to rural folk or low-income people seeking some sense of purpose and solace in the void of the city. Frazier continues:

> In these small "storefront" churches the Negro migrant could worship in a manner to which he had been accustomed . . . The preacher leads the singing of the Spirituals and other hymns with which the Negroes with a folk background are acquainted. The singing is accompanied by "shouting" or holy dancing which permits the maximum of free religious expression on the part of the participants.

Spiritual churches mushroomed in the early twentieth century in northern cities, following black migrations from the South. Anthropologist Hans A. Baer, author of *The Black Spiritual Movement*, says: "The black spiritual movement has syncretized American spiritualism, Afro-American Protestantism, Roman Catholicism and voodoo. How those elements are blended together varies considerably from region to region and city to city—there's a lot of fluidity."

"It's a very eclectic religious movement," continues Baer. "You have middle class people in it, but it came out of the black working class and is still largely a lower-class movement . . . A lot of these churches were coming out of Baptist or Methodist or Pentecostal roots."

Baer considers Black Hawk "central to spiritualism, white or black." Yet in his research among churches in Nashville, New Orleans, Detroit and Chicago, the only Black Hawk services of which he was aware were in New Orleans. There may be Black Hawk services in the other cities, concedes Baer, but he does not know of them.

Nor does Claude Jacobs, who teaches at Oakland University near Detroit, where his research had tracked themes he excavated in the 1970s and early 1980s with Andrew Kaslow for their book, *The Spiritual Churches of New Orleans*.

Jacobs and Kaslow consider the New Orleans churches both a "religious movement" and "a women's movement" because the lines of leadership that followed Leafy Anderson were predominantly female. Although the leadership has shifted more toward men in recent years, the churches remain largely female.

Another scholar who has researched Leafy Anderson's back pages, David Estes, an associate professor of English at Loyola University of New Orleans, consulted Chicago city directories and found her address listed in 1914: "lunch 3114 Federal h. 3128 Federal"—suggesting that she ran a lunch counter several doors down from her residence on the South Side. She is not listed in the directory from 1910 to 1913, or in the one for 1915; however, in 1916 and 1917 her given address is 3021 Federal—she had moved one block. No directory was published from 1918 through 1922.

Picture Leafy in Chicago in her middle twenties: running a short-order grill or sandwich shop on a South Side street teeming with black people, many of them up from the South. Preparing food by day leaves little time for spirits of the night, yet she dug a foothold in a culture that had theretofore been the province of male preachers.

Zora Neale Hurston wrote that Leafy arrived in New Orleans in 1918. Jacobs and Kaslow, who estimate 1919 or 1920, report that she "had begun organizing missions and churches" after she left Chicago in "Little Rock, Memphis, Pensacola, Biloxi, Houston, New Orleans and smaller towns." That is a substantial amount of organizing for an itinerant minister. Something was driving Leafy Anderson, and it was not the Bible.

Teaching people to summon spirits, wearing jewels and fancy dresses, hosting rooftop parties on Amelia Street where people danced the jitterbug, putting jazzmen in her church where white people sometimes sat next to blacks—she exhibited a life-force of rare and dramatic qualities.

A ribbon of cultures ran through working-class neighborhoods where she ministered: Irish, blacks, Italians, and other ethnic groups lived so close together that an inevitable mingling softened the texture of daily life beneath the segregation laws. Yet it was no paradise city for black people. In 1900, a race riot broke out after Robert Charles shot twenty-seven white people, including seven policemen, before dying in a fusillade of police bullets. A white mob killed two blacks in vengeance.

The white police and criminal court constituted a praetorian presence in the lives of black people. Most blacks had no political power and considered police as something to be avoided.

Mother Anderson is remembered for her courage—a memory that may explain why belief in Black Hawk runs so strong. Before obtaining her church charter as required by law, she was arrested and briefly incarcerated. "She had a candle drill," says Bishop Caldwell, referring to the Spiritual tradition of candlelit processions. "She had a march, people were barefoot, and the police didn't allow you to have no marches at that time in the city." She probably had no parade permit.

Others believe the police accused Mother Anderson of practicing medicine without a license. "She got the ministry going down here," says Bishop Efzelda Coleman, a protégée of Lydia Gilford, "and she met a lot of opposition because the authorities felt that she was doing Voodoo."

Bishop Inez Adams, who for many years has held an annual ceremony honoring the founder, told David Estes that Mother Anderson led a "prayer service in the jail, and the walls cracked. When they brought her before the judge, she prophesied to the judge about his invalid child he had at home."

Bishop Edmonia Caldwell picks up the story: "She told the judge, 'You should get to your house. Your baby is sick.' The judge's wife called and said the baby is sick. They rushed the baby to the hospital. She went back and her and the judge talked."

According to Bishop Adams: "She told the judge so many true things about the child, that's how he could turn her loose . . . and told them, don't arrest her no more."

Present-day Spiritual church leaders often cite the allegations of Voodoo activity against Mother Anderson as an example of the persecution she endured in founding the church.

"She wore white cotton robes on her church nights," remarks Bishop Caldwell. "But with seances she was wearing men's suits—black silk suit, white shirt, black tie and a top hat. . . . They tell me she used to have seances on Jackson Avenue to call Black Hawk's spirit."

We can only guess about how much self-recorded information on Leafy lay in her Bible that disappeared in the hurricane flood of 1965. "There's a lot of mysteries in there," reflects Edmonia Caldwell, who carries stories of Leafy from her late uncle, Johnny Davis of Raceland.

Leafy's natural son, George Anderson, left Louisiana years ago, after her death, for parts unknown. She had two adopted children while living in New Orleans—Frank Nelson, who apparently went to Chicago after she died, and a girl named Beatrice (who is not mentioned in the obituaries), "a little baby who was left on her doorstep," says Caldwell. However incomplete some of the information may be, the power of her personality as carried down the years reveals a woman of exceptional tenacity.

"I can understand her," continues Bishop Coleman, who keeps a Black Hawk altar in her home. "It's like if you prepare yourself for a part, you put yourself in that person's personality to be able to portray them, like on the screen, and that's how I see her and Black Hawk. I see her as a person that through her ministry was trying to give belief back, something to believe in, you know, rather than going to the [Catholic] saints. You have to realize the time she lived in and how much oppression had taken place. And so Black Hawk . . . this was a new and a fresh approach to putting a belief value in place."

"She did do a lot of good," says Efzelda Coleman. "She had a lot of, I guess you could call 'em, homes for abused women; she had centers and things that could give people lodging."

There was also speculation about Mother Anderson's sexual orientation. The FWP writer McKinney, whose skepticism colors the interpretive passages he wrote, refers to "rumors that Mother Anderson was a lesbian or man posing as a woman," and then quotes Mother Dora: "Taint true all de things ya hear er bout Mother Anderson. She was much a woman as I is an Ise know Ise a woman every word of it. Ise know cause I nursed her when she was sick. She had a breast lak mine; dere wasn't nuthin' artificial dere, no sir, tak it from me. In de street she wore deep neck dresses to let people see her brest. She was a natural woman."

In any event, the image Leafy Anderson cut was clearly a strong one. "Mother Dora states that Mother Anderson had body guards to keep her safe from abductors," wrote McKinney.

A woman preacher pulling in serious cash, living in a rough neighborhood, had reason to pay for security—abduction, though, was less a threat than mugging.

But the skepticism registered in the manuscript essays of FWP writers cannot be dismissed; a tone of condescension in some of McKinney's comments and those of certain other FWP writers is understandable. They were educated people writing about poor people who believed in healing, exorcism, spirit possessions and prophecies. Some of the interviewees were theatrical to say the least—inspired by Leafy, they made drama of themselves. What writer wouldn't think of it as a little bit whacky?

Perhaps the most stinging criticism of the larger religious movement comes from Joseph Washington, Jr., a respected scholar of religion. In *Black Cults and Sects*, published in 1973, Washington wrote:

> Fundamentally, then, a Spiritualist cult is a house of religious prostitution, where religion is only the means for the end of commercialization. It is a business venture, a pleasure-seeking enterprise. It is tailored for those who are too superstitious to cut themselves off completely from religion, but who seek only its good luck . . . Spiritualists hold out no program for black people, nor do they bother to spend their energies in search of salvation. It is a religion of form without substance which seeks through fears of bad luck a profit in selling good luck.

One need not be an anthropologist to find Washington's assessment unduly harsh when applied to many of the New Orleans churches. By the late 1930s, with the religious movement spreading in New Orleans, the "ist" was dropped from Spiritual, forging a closer link to traditional ideas of God-as-spirit, with Jesus and Catholic saints becoming major figures in the pantheon.

The larger belief system, however alien or even primitive it may seem to the critical mind, is one durable link in a chain of memory connecting believers to the spiritual ethos of a mother culture. This is not to proclaim that all Spiritual ministers are pure of heart. Then again, how many other religions are immunized against charlatans and hypocrites? Jimmy Swaggart's sexual swamp was merely the most spectacular scandal that stained the image of televangelists in the 1980s; the Roman Catholic Church's hundreds of child-molesting clerics cost its hierarchy incalculably more in moral esteem than the $400 million in legal and medical costs.

"Stereotypes often have an element of truth," writes Hans A. Baer in *The Black Spiritual Movement: A Religious Response to Racism*, "but basically they make exaggerated and distorted statements about social reality." The reality here is a religious resistance to a system of racial and economic domination that still falls hard on people of color. "Instances of dubious and fraudulent behavior do occur in Spiritual churches," adds Baer, "but so do they in more respectable groups, not to speak of the highest echelons of the larger society's political, economic and social institutions."

Baer contends that the "more questionable happenings in the Spiritual movement cannot be understood unless we consider the structural position of Blacks in American society.

"The poor," writes the anthropologist in a poignant coda, "have always been forced to live by mother wit in order to survive in a ruthless world that exploits them."

In this respect the most striking aspect of Leafy Anderson's career was the racial chasm she sought to bridge.

Two whites are identified in the FWP accounts as students of Mother Anderson's in 1920. One of them, Lena Scovotto, became one of Leafy's best friends. By 1926 she was Reverend Scovotto, with her own church, Sacred Heart, a few blocks up on Amelia. Born Lena Gandolfo, she was one of thirteen children whose parents had emigrated from Italy. Lena and one of her sisters married two brothers named Scovotto in New Orleans.

Leafy Anderson and Lena Scovotto "were close, like two peas in a pod," recalls her brother, Philip Gandolfo, seventy-seven. "She taught my sister Lena, directed her, helped her to get started in the profession of being a Spiritual. When Mother Anderson got sick, my sister Lena took care of her and so did a lady friend Mother Anderson had, I can't remember her name" (it was probably Dora Tyson).

Although Gandolfo was only nine when Mother Anderson died, he was quite close to Lena, who lived into her eighties. "Lena had the biggest Spiritual Church [Sacred Heart] in New Orleans, on Amelia and Baronne," he says. "She was a highly known woman, a very gifted woman."

"Colored and white went to her church," says a daughter-in-law of the late Reverend Scovotto. The church today is St. Daniel Spiritual Church, where the congregation is black. Bishop Edmonia Cald-well worships there.

According to the *Louisiana Weekly* account of a four-day gather-ing of Spiritualist churches in late 1926, Rev. Lena Scovoto [*sic*], "reporting 75 white members and a host of well-wishers and friends . . . also spoke of how the spirit had worked through her, giving spiritual thanks and greeting to the beloved spirit." Elsewhere, the account notes: "Very good and beautiful points were demonstrated through Rev. Lena Scovoto and our supreme president and beloved pastor, Rev. L. Anderson."

The account of the gathering in late November of 1926—where Leafy performed her "spirit cantata" about the Indian reservation— mentions Becking Light Church, at 3020 Michigan Avenue, Chicago, and the True Light Spiritualist Church of Chicago, at 3842 Eden Avenue, as having sent representatives. "Words of encouragement were spoken to all through the wonderful spirits demonstrating through Mother Anderson," the article states.

The Chicago churches apparently no longer exist; neither does the particular church Leafy Anderson founded in New Orleans. But that November 1926 gathering at her Amelia Street church seems to have been a turning point. From Florida, from the Chicago area, from Houston and New Orleans came ministers, many of whom she had trained. References to people citing scripture are laced through the article by one Rev. M. D. Minor (himself a participant, from Pensa-cola)—the bridge between Spiritualism and Christianity was moving into place.

The various churches reported financial contributions to the Eternal Life Christian Spiritualist Church, which was now anchored in New Orleans—and biracial. Smaller churches in areas where Leafy had proselytized sent messages:

> No. 14, Houston, Texas, Eternal Life Sunset Mission of Independent Heights' message is pray for us that by next year we, too, may become a part of the grand national body . . .
>
> No. 15, Biloxi, Miss., F.I. says remembers us: we are keeping the faith, though just a few in number and without shelter, but we know in time everything will be made all right. Our prayers are God bless Mother Anderson and hasten the day for her to return back us. May the grand and noble work live on.

The New Orleans churches' guiding citation from scripture has come down from the days of Mother Anderson. It is from John 4:24—"God is a spirit and they that worship him must worship him in spirit and in truth."

As the Mardi Gras Indian gangs paid Native Americans the high compliment of adapting the Indian persona, so Mother Anderson, in transplanting a memory of Rock Island's rebel warrior, effectively made Black Hawk a chief, a rank that he never attained in life.

Just when the church movement she launched had begun to grow, Mother Anderson died, on December 12, 1927, after a short bout with the flu. Her last words, reportedly, were: "I am going away but I am coming back and you shall know that I am here."

The obituary said that a niece, Mrs. A. Price Bennett, who had recently been working among victims of the flood that had ravaged the Delta counties straddling the Mississippi River, accompanied the body to Chicago. The article refers to Frank Nelson, her adopted fourteen-year-old son, whose history, like Leafy's burial site, is shrouded in mystery. The death certificate says the body was taken to Chicago.

When Zora Neale Hurston's research on Voodoo brought her to New Orleans in 1928, she attended a service at Leafy's church on Amelia Street. "On Monday nights there is a meeting presided by a woman, which the spirit of Mother Anderson attends," she wrote.

The church soon closed due to financial problems. Today Mother Anderson is invoked in December services by Bishop Inez Adams of the Queen Esther Spiritual Temple. Queen Esther of the Old Testament, another of Leafy's spirit guides, violated tradition by entering the court to save people condemned by a king.

As the various reverend mothers fanned out across the city, preaching in an array of chapels, temples and compounds, the leaders reached for a loftier Christian standard. In a heavily Catholic city, they anointed one another as bishops and archbishops. As the movement grew, it split in several organizational directions. The wing that honors Mother Anderson and Black Hawk most often is led by Archbishop E. J. Johnson of the Israelite Divine Spiritual Church on Frenchmen Street.

Thus did Black Hawk become a mythic figure on the stage of ritual memory. He joins a gathering of spirits. See them now, like dancers in a ring: the Bambara and Indians who harbored slaves; Papa Legba and the Fon, Eshu-Elegba and the Yoruba; the dancers, drummers and banjo precursors of Congo Square; Marie Laveau and the Voodoo cultists; now the Big Chief and Spy Boys and skeletons of Carnival; now Leafy, now Queen Esther, now Mother Catherine, taking in battered women and unwed mothers, all of them raising a cry to heaven and the gods, *a cry for justice.*

BLACK HAWK

IN TIME

Black Hawk celebration, 9 December 1994; photograph by Syndey
Byrd

Above the altar of the Israelite Divine Spiritual Church hangs a framed photograph of the pastor, Archbishop E. J. Johnson, wearing a mitre. He is now eighty-eight years old; the lettering along the frame, which reads "Happy 64th Anniversary," acknowledges his years in the garden of the faith.

Archbishop Johnson does not look his age; a sturdy man with a clarion baritone and smooth-spoken cadences, he welcomes the faithful this "first Friday" night for an annual Black Hawk service.

A long table occupies the central isle, meeting a horizontal table spanning the length of the altar. The T-shaped table is laden with bananas, sugarcane stalks, sweet potatoes, apples, oranges and peppermints, interspersed with trio-clusters of red candles. The plaster bust of an Indian sits at the T of the table. From the kitchen off the foyer of the church wafts the succulent aroma of a basting turkey. A feast night in a Spiritual church offers food to the faithful.

Archbishop Johnson says he did not know Mother Anderson, though he joined the religion just before she died. Christened Catholic, he attended Protestant churches as a youth.

"When I visited the Spiritual Church for the first time," he told folklorist Alan Govenar, "I had an afflicted arm. My arm was swollen. For two weeks I had been unable to use it. The first time I went they prayed for me and laid a hand on my arm, and the next day my arm was normal as it's supposed to be. From there I picked up faith and began following until I was converted." He was ordained in 1927. "We were in rented halls and things like that. I did that for three years and then in 1930 I bought a church called Israelite Spiritual Church at 631 Roman Street. We stayed there thirty-five, maybe forty years, until the highway came and took that. We got this church in May of 1970."

The service opens with an alteration of the Catholic Nicene Creed: "We believe that God is a spirit," the prayer begins, ". . . and in Jesus Christ, who sits at the right hand of the father."

The faithful continue: "We believe in the Holy Ghost, the Divine Spiritual Church, the communion of saints, the forgiveness of sins, the resurrection of the body . . ."

On the altar stand statues of the Virgin Mary and the Infant Jesus of Prague, opposite the figure of a bearded Jesus. Small balconies on opposite sides of the altar feature statues of Jesus with shepherd's staff surrounded by eight candles sheathed in red glass.

The next prayer is the Our Father.

Archbishop Johnson in his red robe sits at the organ, laying down a syncopated rhythm, punctuated by the rattling claps of a tambourine held by Bishop Oliver Johnson, a tall, compact man wearing a maroon robe.

Of the thirty people here tonight, most are women; in the pew behind me sit two girls, about ten and eight, with a boy about six. The singing continues, with "Amazing Grace" leading into "Praise Him."

From the organ, Archbishop Johnson says: "We came out tonight to have a good time—to give God the Glory. We came out to honor Black Hawk tonight!"

"Yes-Lawd!"

A collection is taken. Then another gospel song, "By and By," is sung.

The archbishop is at the pulpit. "Truly we will understand it better by and by. Receive Him by raising our right hand and saying amen."

"Amen," say the congregants, hands aloft.

"We give glory to God—to our entire staff," says Archbishop Johnson. "We come down to the spirit of Black Hawk. Black Hawk is just all right!"

"*Yes he is,*" comes a voice from the pew.

"God got a way to bring his people out!" the pastor continues. "Somebody might be here tonight and they may not understand why we shout, why we give admiration and honor to Black Hawk. But God is a spirit, hallelujah!"

"*Hallelujah!*"

"And they that worship him must worship him in spirit and in truth . . ."

Bishop Oliver Coleman, a paralegal and spiritual counselor,

takes the floor. Says he: "I'm just excited about this because not very long ago I didn't know too much about this—I didn't know who Black Hawk was. But it was one evening around the corner from here, when I just lived on Treasure Street, I was in meditation. I was trying to make a decision about which direction to take my ministry in. I had talked to Bishop Griffin, he was one of my mentors, God bless him, he's gone on now, but I thank God for him tonight.

"I talked to the late Mother Adleide . . . We talked about the spirit. We talked about Saint Anthony, we talked about Saint Michael, we talked about Raphael and the other saints. But then we talked about Black Hawk!"

"Ohhh-yesss!"

"And one thing I remember Mother Smith said to me: 'You will never know about him till you meet him for yourself.' "

"Awright," says Archbishop Johnson approvingly.

"Then one evening I was in my room," continues Oliver Coleman, whose wife Efzelda is also a bishop. "I was trying to make a decision, I kept feeling a presence in my room. And I said what's goin' on here? I was doing the *Gospel News Magazine,* just typing away, I heard a voice speaking—I saw something but I didn't really know what I was seeing—"

"That's *all right,*" says the archbishop in an avuncular tone.

A voice, continues Coleman, spoke to him: " 'Me come to help you. Me Black Hawk: me come to help you!' "

The organ cuts a long slur as he speaks of a bishop who warned him not to burn too many candles in his house. But, says Coleman, "Truly I've been burning candles ever since!"

The organ zooms, hands clap.

"I've been working with the spirit of Black Hawk with clients ever since . . . I know it's a greater force. I believe in God 'cause he is a spirit, and if we ask—"

Zoom comes the organ like a shooting star.

"I come to tell you tonight if you are going through a battle, the word of God say stand still and see the salvation. And I want to tell you I don't know who may come! But if you're in trouble, and got a battle and ask Him to send *him*, if Black Hawk comes, *you'll know it!* You'll hear the rumbling, the beat, and you'll know the deliverance: the help is on the way.

"God bless you," concludes Oliver Coleman, "and for each of you I'm praying. I'm so glad he'll make a way for you."

Another man is on the organ, playing a slow tempo that rocks along like a 1950s rhythm-and-blues song, with tambourines jangling as people sing:

> *He'll fight your battles*
> *He's on the wall*
> *He's on the wall*
> *He's a mighty good watchman*
>   *On the wall!*
> *He's a mighty good warrior*
>   *On the wall!*

He's a mighty good leader
  On the wall
He's a mighty good watchman
  On the wall
He's a mighty good battler
  On the wall
He's a mighty good warrior
  On the wall . . . on the wall.

Archbishop Johnson takes the podium. "Bishop Coleman, we heard about Black Hawk," he says in the gently rolling baritone.

"Yes, he's a watchman on the wall. If you got a *problem*, he'll work it out for you."

The pastor invites believers to testify. Scanning the room, I realize how small the gathering is tonight. A question among those who study the churches is whether a new generation will draw more believers.

Another man stands at the pulpit. "First giving honor to Archbishop Johnson," he says. Black Hawk "is a saint that God uses. He's a marvelous saint and he works miracles. I'm glad to be part of the feast of Black Hawk."

It seems that Black Hawk has overtaken the memory of Mother Anderson as a leading spirit guide—or is this merely the speculation of an outsider?

The worshippers sing "The Battle Hymn of the Republic," after which the pastor says, "Thank you! Give *God* a *good* hand!" And the people erupt in applause.

"Amen!" says the archbishop.

"Tonight I'm so happy to be here," says another man, addressing Bishop Inez Adams, seated on the altar in her mauve robe, her head gently swaying to the organ's hum.

"To Bishop Adams, to all our Christian friends," the man continues, "I am one of those that at one time the spirit of Father Black Hawk did come to me!"

"Amen!" cries Archbishop Johnson.

"I know that he's a watchman on the wall!" he continues, speaking now of a trip he made to Rock Island. "And I saw the big statue of Black Hawk. I know that there is a power . . . I always said Indians were great people for fasting and praying and working with the spirit."

The tambourine rattles, someone claps.

"In this life in which we live, conditions may become so strong that we can't handle the situation. We need somebody to come along and push a way, make a way out of nowhere—"

"Oh yessss . . ."

"All right!"

"And Father Black Hawk is that person. I call upon him. I give him honor."

The organ hums a warm electronic purr and the shaking tambourines reverberate as a man sings: "I heard the Lord singing, yeah-heah . . ."—stretching out the syllables—"I heard the spirit sayin', yeahh-ah-hannn-heahhh, ohhh, ohhhhh, oh-yeahhhh! I came to *praise the Lord!*"

Now Bishop Inez Adams stands at the podium. The Queen Esther Spiritual Temple is part of her house, several miles away in the lower Ninth Ward. Her next-door neighbor is Fats Domino, who has a big pink house and a smaller shotgun house side by side. The wooden statue of an angel stands on her front porch, a studied contrast to the gold-and-black color scheme of Fats's shotgun cottage, surrounded by Quaid fence, a hundred yards away.

She tells the people about her thoughts of an hour or so earlier. "As I lay down in my bed it's almost 7:30, it don't look like I'm gonna make it tonight and you know I wanna go!" But the spirit moved her and she made it.

"*Awright!*" responds Archbishop Johnson.

"I can tell you a whole lot about these spirit guides!" she cries.

"Yessuh!" comes a man's voice.

Inez Adams: "There was times when my back was against the *wall!*"

"*Oh yeah!*" cries the pastor.

"I heard Him askin' me tonight—"

Crack! goes the tambourine.

"When I asked Him questions, I could hear the spirit say yeah! Now you got to learn to ask Him questions . . ."

Bishop Adams is singing:

> I heard the Lord singing, *Yeahhhh*
> *IIIIII heard the Lord singing, yeah-he-yay-ya*
> I heard the Lord *this morning* saying, yeh-oh-ohhhohhh
> Children *oh-yeahhhh* . . .

Now the organist begins a processional beat, the melody moving, weaving, meandering ahead. "I don't know about you, but I feel like it's saying *yes* to me!" Bishop Adams cries buoyantly. "I got a *feeling* that everything is gonna be all right. Thank you, Lord!"

"Hallelujah!"

The music lowers, and a feeling of calm descends upon the room as Bishop Adams says, "We gonna bring our own archbishop to you. You better say amen."

"Amen!"

"Amen!"

People clap, the organ hums beneath the pastor's fingers and Archbishop Johnson sings: "Ohh, the light, shining in my soul, ohhh, Jesus is the light, the light of the world, Jesus is the light, of the world . . ."

Then he takes the podium.

"God bless you. First obedience to Father God and Son Jesus, bishops, ministers, members and friends," he says mellifluously. "It's good to be here tonight. Give God the praise. Let's say amen."

Another man plays the organ as people say "amen."

"And with Black Hawk, we're still giving God the praise. Cuz He is the powerhouse. Without Him nothing can be done. Through Him, we can accomplish whatever we desire."

To the gently pleading chords of the organ, he speaks words that, read cold on the printed page, suggest a fiery fundamentalism. But the rhythms and gentleness of his cadences, the sound of the voice gives a different timbre to the Word.

"Lot of people don't understand that in this life we're not just flesh and blood. There are powers and principalities. Satan got an army out there and his army is to defeat *you* . . . and defeat me. And God has an army out there, a spiritual force and there is a war going on and sometime that war go on within you. Satan tryin' to get you to do one thing and the Lord intend us do something else. And one thing about it, he give us a lil wisdom and lil knowledge to know right from wrong. We do our wrongs sometime and then we be knowing we doing wrong and when we do that wrong we got to pay for it. You'll forgive us, but we got to pay for it. Someway or other you got to pay for the deeds that are happening."

He gestures to the bust of Black Hawk surrounded by fruit and candles on the table. "And a lot of folk think we are worshippin' the statue. But it's not the statue—we got a spirit goal. God said, 'So you live, so you die.' If you live a good life, you'll be a good spirit."

"Ohh, Lawwd," a woman moans as the organ hums.

"If you die a liar digging pits, that's what you goan be doin' [in the next world]—digging pits and lying. Earthbound spirit. Let's say amen."

"Amen!"

"But we thank God that we lookin to the hill from when come Thy help. Our help come from the Lord which made heaven and earth. Black Hawk was a great warrior," he continues in his calm oracular rhythm. "He fought for his right and he'll do the same for you. I heard a line, 'Work with him!'"

Now, in reference to Rock Island, he says, "I went up to the monument, a big statue as tall as this building. Let's say amen. And people are going there all day, all through the years. They must find some kind of favor because they wouldn't be doing it for nothing."

A calmness shrouds the room like the gray light on a summer day, just before rain, when time seems to stand still.

"One thing about it, your faith makes you whole. If you believe it, then God'll bring it to pass. But you got to first believe . . . And this is a great feast that Bishop Adams started and we been trying to carry it on ever since. It's a blessing in these feasts. If we go through the Bible we find there are many feasts and many blessings came from them. Out of the feast a whole nation was saved!"

The organ notes dip now, ever gently.

"The feast mean you give something back that God has given you. A lot of hands have gone into this table. It isn't as huge as we usually have it. But the Lord is good and His mercies will go forever."

As he calls the people to a consecration prayer, Archbishop Johnson says, "The table's been blessed and we want to ask the Lord, who is good and able to to give you the desires of your heart."

A woman testifies, riffing off the Lord's Prayer as the children in the pew behind me begin to squirm. The organ peals a peaceful line as the archbishop says, "We're going to sell our lights and oil. It's seven dollars. If you don't want the lights, you can get the oil. If you don't want the oil, don't matter. But believe God can work it out for you. You ever had a problem, God can solve it. Say amen."

Filing down the table, laden with food, I think of the candles I have lit in Catholic churches, dropping money into a slot. In this church you buy the candle and take it home.

A woman announces, "It's a custom whenever we consecrate a table, we ask for offering. Give something, if it's no more than a silver dime."

As people offer their dollars and silver coins, the woman says, "I could stand up all night and tell you the things that Father Black Hawk has worked out for me. I asked God to help him, ask him to offer my petition to God, and I've never asked him to do something he didn't do."

After the service we file into the foyer where Archbishop Johnson presents each person with a covered Styrofoam plate, packed with turkey, dressing, cranberry sauce and string beans.

Thanking the archbishop and other members of the church, I step into the brisk December night, thinking of Leafy Anderson. How little I know of her, and yet how much.

Somewhere in this continent's buried dreams, the memory of Black Hawk found its own spirit guide in Leafy. And I suppose it is fitting that the point of contact between them remains a mystery, something the Spiritual followers accept as a seed that has borne fruits of the faith. Maybe it is the rusty memory of my own boyhood— those Latin chants and supernatural tales of miracles and mystics the nuns imparted—that leaves me thinking, against the dictates of history, that perhaps we are better off not knowing the full answer. Perhaps in summoning Black Hawk Mother Leafy Anderson wanted a spiritual drama guaranteed to manifest itself in the hearts and minds of her followers. At that she did succeed. Mostly black, mostly women, saddled with hardship and struggle, they embraced her, and him, as spirit guides and saints guarding the rock of ages.

NOTES

MOVEMENTS OF THE SPIRIT

p. 9   "The documentary . . ." Jason Berry and Jonathan Foose, *Up From the Cradle of Jazz* (WYES, LPB, 1980: distributed by Center for the Study of Southern Culture, University of Mississippi, Oxford, Mississippi).

p. 12   "I endured the rebukes and scorns . . ." Jason Berry, Jonathan Foose, and Tad Jones, *Up From the Cradle of Jazz: New Orleans Music Since World War II* (Athens: University of Georgia Press, 1986), 42.

pp. 12–13   Mother Catherine Seals information: Claude F. Jacobs and Andrew J. Kaslow, *The Spiritual Churches of New Orleans: Origins, Beliefs and Rituals of an African-American Religion* (Knoxville: University of Tennessee Press, 1991), 40. See also Lyle Saxon, Robert Tallant and Edward Dreyer, *Gumbo Ya-Ya: A Collection of Louisiana Folk Tales* (New York: Bonanza Books, 1945), 209.

p. 13   "Mother Catherine was not converted . . ." Zora Neale Hurston, "Mother Catherine" from Nancy Cunard, editor; abridged, Hugh Ford, *Negro: An Anthology* (New York: Frederick Ungar, 1970), 40, 42.

p. 15   Jacobs and Kaslow, *Spiritual Churches*, 41.

p. 18   Interview with Jules Anderson, October 29, 1983. Portions of the interview appeared in articles by the author: "The Spirit of Black Hawk," *New Orleans Magazine*, March 1984; same title, *Chicago Reader*, July 3, 1994.

BLACK HAWK IN HISTORY

p. 25   "I was born . . ." Donald Jackson, ed., *Black Hawk: An Autobiography* (Urbana: University of Illinois Press, 1955), 47. The cover of the original work, with the title *Life of Ma-Ka-Tai-Me-She-Kia-Kiak or Black Hawk*, is reproduced on page 39.

p. 25   "Black Hawk's story . . ." Ibid., 37.

p. 26   For description of the village and historical background on the Sauk, the Fox and events that shaped the Black Hawk War, I have relied on Donald Jackson's introduction to *Black Hawk*; Reuben G. Thwaites, *The Story of Wisconsin* (Boston: Lathrop, 1899); two articles in the summer 1982 *Wisconsin Magazine of History* (published by the State Historical Society of Wisconsin): "The Black Hawk War in Retrospect" by Roger L. Nichols, 239–45, and "Prelude to Disaster: The Course of Indian-White Relations Which Led to the Black Hawk War of 1832" by Anthony F. C. Wallace, 247–88; and an article in the summer 1988 edition of that magazine by Nancy Oestreich Lurie, "In Search of Chaetar: New Findings on Black Hawk's Surrender."

p. 26   "Standing by my father's side . . ." Jackson, *Black Hawk*, 53.

p. 27   "I blacked my face . . ." Ibid., 55–56.

p. 27   "Hunting grounds during . . ." Wallace, *Wisconsin Magazine of History*, 254.

p. 29   "But a crucial difference . . ." Ibid.

p. 29   "one of our people . . ." Jackson, *Black Hawk*, 60.

p. 29   "some white settlers . . ." Wallace, *Wisconsin Magazine of History*, 261.

p. 30   "According to Wallace . . ." Ibid.

p. 30   "paying for the person killed . . ." Jackson, *Black Hawk*, 60.

p. 31   "on the west . . ." and "had been drunk . . ." Ibid., 61.

p. 31   On 1804 treaty: Wallace, *Wisconsin Magazine of History*, 257–60.

p. 32   "He passionately hated . . ." Thwaites, *Story of Wisconsin*, 182.

p. 32   "As Black Hawk told . . ." and "Why did the Great . . ." Jackson, *Black Hawk*, 68–69.

p. 34   "With the Indian Removal Act . . ." Peter H. Wood, "When Old Worlds Meet: Southern Indians Since Columbus," *Southern Exposure* (spring 1992).

p. 36   "I now determined . . ." Jackson, *Black Hawk*, 124; "There was no . . ." Ibid., 113.

p. 37   "Their village . . ." *The Aboriginal Races of North America* by Samuel Drake (New York: Hurst, 1880), p. 643.

p. 38   "In his memoir . . ." Jackson, *Black Hawk*, 119.

p. 38   "The immediate aftermath . . ." Wallace, *Wisconsin Magazine of History*, 276.

p. 40   "The dead that were found . . ." *Aboriginal Races*, 645.

p. 41   "With consummate skill . . ." Thwaites, *Story of Wisconsin*, 188.

p. 42   "They tried . . ." Jackson, *Black Hawk*, 35.

p. 43   "On our way . . ." Ibid., 164–65.

p. 43   "a forlorn crew . . ." Jackson, introduction, Ibid., 9n.

p. 43   "Chief Keokuk . . ." Katharine C. Turner, *Red Men Calling on the Great White Father* (Norman: University of Oklahoma Press, 1951), 89.

p. 44   " 'wonderful' road . . ." Jackson, *Black Hawk*, 169.

p. 44   Turner, *Red Men*, 90.

p. 45   "had seen as many winters . . ." Jackson, *Black Hawk*, 170.

p. 45   "It is only necessary . . ." Turner, *Red Men*, 91.

p. 45   "the Great Spirit of myself . . ." Ibid., 91–92.

p. 45   "I am a man and you are another" Ibid., 92.

pp. 45–46   quotations from Turner, citing New York *American*.

p. 46   "Katharine C. Turner . . ." *Red Men*, 93.

p. 47   "raising the tomahawk . . ." Ibid., 96. Katharine Turner also writes that Black Hawk, after the president's request that they cease "raising the tomahawk," replied: "The tomahawk has been buried so deep that it would never be resurrected." The Indian's quotation in Turner's footnote credits the Black Hawk memoir that was republished in 1882 by John Patterson, the newspaper publisher who had worked with Antoine LeClaire on the original manuscript dictated by the Indian. The quotation in question, however, does not appear in the original 1833 edition, which was republished in 1955, with Donald Jackson's introduction and footnotes. "Patterson added material," says anthropologist Nancy Lurie, "and he was inclined to flowery language."

p. 47   "A newspaper speculated . . ." *U.S. Telegraph*; Turner, *Red Men*, 96.

pp. 47–48   "the only disappointment . . ." Ibid., 97. "I think he can go to the heavens . . ." Ibid., 98.

p. 48   "He would not . . ." Ibid., 97.

p. 48   "making a monkey . . ." Ibid., 98.

p. 48   "dressed in a short blue frock coat . . ." Jackson, introduction, *Black Hawk*, 17.

p. 49   "The old man rose . . ." Jackson, *Black Hawk*, 176, fn.

pp. 50–51   John Latrobe, *Southern Travels: Journal of John Latrobe 1834*, edited and with an introduction by Samuel Wilson, Jr. (New Orleans: The Historic New Orleans Collection, 1986), 75.

p. 52   "I was once a great warrior . . ." Jackson, *Black Hawk*, epilogue, 181.

p. 52   ". . . obtained Black Hawk's skeleton . . ." Dee Brown, *Bury My Heart at Wounded Knee* (New York: Holt, 1970), 5.

THE WORLD OF LEAFY ANDERSON

pp. 56–59   The photograph of Mother Anderson was on the altar of Archbishop B. S. Johnson, who was photographed in 1974 by Michael P. Smith. He enlarged the picture of Mother Anderson for the image that appears in this book.

Description of Leafy Anderson and information on her early locations come from Robert McKinney, "Mother Letha or Lefy Anderson" [*sic*]—(Mother Dora Tyson) an interview-report for the Federal Writers Project, the Robert Tallant Collection, New Orleans Public Library, 1–3, and from *The Spiritual Churches of New Orleans*, 32–36.

Hereafter all such manuscripts are referred to as Tallant Collection, NOPL.

The manuscripts of interviews with Spiritualist figures vary considerably in accuracy of spelling and quality of typing; conducted in the 1930s, many of the summaries are undated. As field reports they are historically quite valuable; however, opinions of the writers often betray bias toward a given interviewee or the larger topic of Spiritualism and the churches. p. 48—"She taught her students . . ." McKinney, Ibid., 2.

p. 59   church description, from an advertisement with photograph of the church that appeared in the *Louisiana Weekly*, December 11, 1926.

p. 60   "Bessie Johnson, told . . ." Michael P. Smith, *Spirit World: Photographs and Journal* (Gretna, LA: Pelican Publishing Co. 1992), 43.

p. 60   "The Life . . ." "Eternal Life Church Presents Play," *Louisiana Weekly*, January 22, 1927.

p. 61   "The conference included . . ." Rev. W. D. Minor, "Eternal Life Spiritualists in Convention," *Louisiana Weekly*, December 4, 1926.

p. 62 "Jesus as a man . . ." Zora Neale Hurston, "Hoodoo in America," *Journal of American Folklore* 44 (October–December, 1931): 321.

p. 62 McKinney, Mother Dora interview, 3.

p. 62 On Chris Kelly: Al Rose and Edmond Souchon, *New Orleans Jazz: A Family Album* (Baton Rouge: Louisiana State University Press, 1967), 66.

p. 63 McKinney, Ibid.

p. 64 Re white churchman and "spirit cantata . . ." The *Louisiana Weekly* article of January 22, 1927, does not bear a byline; given the personality of Leafy Anderson, one can assume that her hand shaped much of its content. The white minister from Lily Dale, New York, is identified as Rev. F. Robertson.

p. 65 "Going back two generations . . ." Tom Dent, interview with author, March 9, 1995.

p. 66 "Mother Anderson's obituary . . ." See "City Shocked By Death of Spiritualist," December 15, 1927. Brief death notices appeared on December 13 in the *Times-Picayune* and *Morning Tribune*.

p. 66 "had their little churches . . ." David Estes, "Ritual Validations of Clergywomen's Authority in the African American Spiritual Churches of New Orleans," in *Women's Leadership in Marginal Religions: Explorations Outside the Mainstream*, ed. Catherine Wessinger (Urbana: University of Illinois Press, 1993), 158.

pp. 66–67 Edmonia Caldwell, interview with author, April 13, 1995.

p. 68 "walked from Virginia . . ." Ibid., 158.

p. 69 "rebellion against death . . ." Ann Braude, *Radical Spirits: Spiritualism and Women's Rights in Nineteenth-Century America* (Boston: Beacon Press, 1989), 56.

p. 69 "dominating, messianic preachers." See Hans A. Baer, *The Black Spiritual Church Movement: A Religious Response to Racism* (Knoxville: University of Tennessee Press, 1984).

p. 69   "When Mother Anderson first came . . ." Robert McKinney, "Saint Black Hawk—Indian Worshipped by Spiritualists," 1, Tallant Collection, NOPL.

p. 70   "the great guiding spirit . . ." McKinney, "Mother Lethe or Lefy Anderson," 3.

p. 70   "It's like when you hear . . ." Smith, *Spirit World*, 43. "Spirit guides can be adopted . . ." Ibid., 43.

p. 72   "It was Leaf Anderson . . ." Ibid.

p. 72   "Archbishop Johnson . . ." Ibid., 45.

p. 73   "We are living happy together . . ." Photocopy of Mother Catherine's will, a two-page autobiographical document she dictated to typist E. M. Barnett, is filed in Civil District Court of Orleans Parish (File # 188001), dated October 11, 1929.

p. 73   "She was always taking people in . . ." Hazel Breaux, "Mother Catherine, Interview with Mrs. Fuccich, 814 Dauphine Street." Mrs. Fuccich's first name is not given. Tallant Collection, NOPL.

p. 76   "Her profession was a wash-woman . . ." Robert McKinney, "When the Thunder is Over Mother Kate Francis Will March Right Through Hebbin's Doors," November 1939, 2–3, Tallant Collection, NOPL.

p. 77   "known to many . . ." Ibid., 1.

p. 77   "Leafy Anderson often said . . ." Interview with author. "The Spirit of Black Hawk," *Chicago Reader*, July 3, 1994.

p. 78   "At the end . . ." Jackson, *Black Hawk*, 179.

p. 79   "he is behaving . . ." Nancy Lurie, telephone interview, March 13, 1995.

p. 80   "With two plantations and fifty slaves . . ." Gwendolyn Medlo Hall, *Africans in Colonial Louisiana: The Development of Afro-Creole Culture in the Eighteenth Century* (Baton Rouge: Louisiana State University Press, 1992), 67.

p. 80   "A special police force . . ." Ibid., 6.

p. 81   "Because most African slaves . . ." Jerah Johnson, "New Orleans's Congo Square: An Urban Setting for Early Afro-American Culture Formation," *Louisiana History* (spring 1991): 127.

p. 81   "The French shipped . . ." Hall, *Africans in Colonial Louisiana*, 72, 77.

p. 82   "transmigration of souls . . ." Ibid., 50.

p. 82   "some twenty-four thousand Indians lived . . ." Wood, *Southern Exposure*, 30. "The water was troubled . . ." Ibid.

p. 83   "The dead were respected . . ." Fred B. Kniffen, Hiram F. Gregory, and George A. Stokes, *The Historic Indian Tribes of Louisiana: From 1542 to the Present* (Baton Rouge: Louisiana State University Press, 1987), 253, 255.

p. 84   "In 1729 . . ." See *Negro Insurrections*, vol. 2 of *Louisiana*, ed. Alcee Fortier (Madison: University of Wisconsin Press, 1914), 213; Henry E. Chambers, *A History of Louisiana*, vol. 1 (Chicago and New York: American Historical Society, 1925), 209–11; Wood, *Southern Exposure*, 31.

p. 84   "The greatest misfortune . . ." Hall, *Africans in Colonial Louisiana*, 103.

p. 86   "To the Yoruba . . ." N. A. Fadipe, *The Sociology of the Yoruba* (Ibadan, Nigeria: Ibadan University Press, 1970) 262.

p. 87   "We can insist . . ." Wole Soyinka, *Myth, Literature and the African World* (New York: Cambridge University Press, 1976), 10.

p. 87   "Nothing is more to be dreaded . . ." Dena J. Epstein, *Sinful Tunes and Spirituals: Black Folk Music to the Civil War* (Urbana: University of Illinois Press, 1976), 32.

p. 87   Francis Bebey, *African Music: A People's Art* (Westport, Conn.: Lawrence Nelson, 1980), 116.

p. 89   "cultural passageways . . ." See Herbert Gutman, *The Black Family in Slavery and Freedom, 1750–1925* (New York: Pantheon, 1977).

p. 89   "Police regulations . . ." Carl Brasseaux, "The Administration of Slave Regulations in French Louisiana, 1724–1766," *Louisiana History* (spring 1980): 155.

p. 90   "*vodun* of the Fon-speaking people . . ." Melville Herskovits, *Life in a Haitian Valley* (Garden City: Doubleday, 1971), 23.

p. 91   "Africa *reblended* . . ." Robert Farris Thompson, *Flash of the Spirit: African and Afro-American Art and Philosophy* (New York: Vintage, 1984), 164.

p. 91   On Eshu-Elegba: Thompson, *Flash of the Spirit*, 18–42.

p. 91   "Legba is the wild card . . ." Henry Louis Gates, Jr., *The Signifying Monkey: A Theory of African-American Literary Criticism* (New York: Oxford University Press, 1988), 23.

p. 91   "Each god speaks . . ." Ibid., 28.

p. 92   "The tradition . . ." Thompson, *Flash of the Spirit*, 25.

p. 92   on Congo Square: Jason Berry, "African Cultural Memory in New Orleans Music," *Black Music Research Journal* 8 (1988); Berry, Foose, Jones, *Cradle of Jazz*; Epstein, *Sinful Tunes and Spirituals*; Johnson, *Louisiana History*; Michael P. Smith, *Mardi Gras Indians* (Gretna, LA: Pelican, 1994).

p. 93   "would make the lives . . ." Robert Tallant, *Voodoo in New Orleans* (Gretna, LA: Pelican, 1994), 9; Hall, *Africans in Colonial Louisiana*, 182.

p. 93   "The ring shout . . ." Sterling Stuckey, *Slave Culture: Nationalist Theory and the Foundations of Black America* (New York: Oxford University Press, 1987), 16.

p. 93   "holy dance . . ." Samuel A. Floyd, Jr., "Ring Shout!" Literary Studies, Historical Studies, and Black Music Inquiry, *Black Music*

Research Journal 2, no. 20 (1991): 266. Floyd develops this theory further in *The Power of Black Music: Interpreting Its History from Africa to the United States* (New York: Oxford University Press, forthcoming in 1995).

p. 94   " 'outside accounts' and several interviews . . ." Tallant, *Voodoo in New Orleans*.

p. 95   "flawed by a racial paternalism . . . near-tabloid obsession with sex . . ." It would be unfair to call Tallant racist. On page 4 of *Voodoo*, he writes: "If [the white man] is at all intelligent and has had many contacts with Negroes he does not believe them to be 'the happiest people on earth.' He does not think of them as being 'funny.' He knows their world is not a minstrel show. He knows they suffer a great deal, that many of them are poor and that they like being poor no more than do persons of his own race." Yet his descriptions of reconstructed Voodoo rites, as on page 8 (to cite but one example) betray the shaky hand of a novelist out of his league: "They bit and clawed at each other. Their scanty garments ripped away. The clouds broke and the moon came out and glowed upon naked black flesh. In pairs they fell upon the hot earth, still panting and gyrating. Some fell unconscious and were dragged away, into the deep darkness of the trees that edged the clearing.

"That is the way it was. At least that is the way we are told it was." At least that is how Tallant thought it was.

p. 96   "Newspaper reporters . . ." Tallant, *Voodoo*, 53. "Marie never lessened in any way . . ." Ibid., 55.

p. 97   "took charge of . . ." Ibid., 56.

p. 98   "Doctor Jim . . ." Ibid., 108.

p. 99   "Papa Legba/ open the gate . . ." Jacobs and Kaslow, *Spiritual Churches*, 84.

p. 100 "an altar in the home . . ." Ibid., 85.

p. 101 *kumina*: Edward Kamau Brathwaite, "The Spirit of African Survival in Jamaica," *Jamaica Journal* 42 (September 1978): 46.

p. 103 "Carnival was a celebration . . . Caribbean," see Berry, Foose, and Jones, *Cradle of Jazz*, chapter 17; Smith, *Mardi Gras Indians*.

p. 105 "whooping red devils . . ." Smith, Ibid., 96.

p. 105 "(as a diary passage suggests) . . ." Berry, Foose, and Jones, *Cradle of Jazz*, 211. The unpublished memoir by Elise Kirsch, *Downtown New Orleans in the Early Eighties: Customs and Characters of Old Robertson Street and Its Neighborhoods* (1951), is in the New Orleans Public Library.

p. 106 "When a Spy Boy . . ." Alan Lomax, *Mister Jelly Roll* (Berkeley: University of California Press, 1950), 15.

p. 107 Berry, Foose, and Jones, *Cradle of Jazz*, 212.

p. 107 "men who'd walk the streets . . ." Ibid., 212.

p. 107 "We were going uptown . . ." Andrew Kaslow, "Folklore: Talking to Some Glorious Mardi Gras Indians," *Figaro* (New Orleans Weekly), February 1, 1976; Berry, Foose, and Jones, *Cradle of Jazz*, 214.

p. 108 "We used to fight . . ." Berry, Foose, and Jones, *Cradle of Jazz*, 216.

p. 109 "If the Indians serve God . . ." Michael P. Smith, *A Joyful Noise: A Celebration of New Orleans Music*, introduction and interviews by Alan Govenar (Dallas: Taylor Publishing Co. 1990), 153.

p. 110 "They want a church . . ." E. Franklin Frazier, *The Negro Church in America* (New York: Schocken, 1974), 58–59.

p. 110 "Anthropologist Hans A. Baer . . ." Telephone interview with the author for *Chicago Reader*. See also Baer, *The Black Spiritual Church Movement*.

p. 111 "consulted Chicago city directories." Courtesy of David Estes.

p. 112   "had begun organizing . . ." Jacobs and Kaslow, *Spiritual Churches*, 33.

p. 112   "no paradise city . . ." See William Ivy Hair, *Carnival of Fury: Robert Charles and the New Orleans Race Riot of 1900* (Baton Rouge: Louisiana State University Press, 1976).

p. 113   "She got the ministry . . ." Bishop Efzelda Coleman, interview with author, January 21, 1995.

p. 113   "prayer service . . ." Estes, *Women's Leadership*, 158.

p. 115   "rumors . . . was a lesbian . . ." McKinney, "Mother Lethe," 3, Tallant Collection, NOPL.

p. 116   Washington quote: see Baer, *The Black Spiritual Church Movement*, 10.

p. 117   "$400 million in . . . costs . . ." See Jason Berry, *Lead Us Not Into Temptation: Catholic Priests and the Sexual Abuse of Children* (New York: Doubleday, 1992).

p. 117   "Stereotypes often have . . ." Baer, *The Black Spiritual Church Movement*, 10–11.

p. 118   "two peas in a pod . . ." Philip Gondolfo, interview with author, February 21, 1995.

p. 118   "Colored and white . . ." confidential communication.

p. 119   "reporting 75 white members . . ." Rev. W. D. Minor, "Eternal Life Spiritualists in Convention," *Louisiana Weekly*, December 4, 1926.

p. 120   "Her last words . . ." as quoted in the *Louisiana Weekly* obituary of December 15, 1927.

p. 121   Hurston, *Journal of American Folklore*, 321.

BLACK HAWK IN TIME

p. 126   "When I visited . . ." Smith and Govenar, *Joyful Noise*, 163.

INDEX

Senegambia, 81–82
Seventh Ward, 106
Sicilians, 102
Sioux Indians, 33, 34–35, 41, 42
Sitting Bull, 21, 22
Slave Culture (Stuckey), 93
Slaves, 79, 80, 81–82, 84, 87, 88, 89, 90, 93–94, 122
Smith, Adleide, 128
Smith, Michael P., 60, 70, 72, 104–05
Souchon, Edmond, 63
Southern Travels, 50–51, 52
Soyinka, Wole, 87
Spanish colonialism in Louisiana, 93
Spirit guides, 6–7, 18–19, 20–22, 61–62, 65, 68–70, 72, 77–78, 121–22, 128–29, 132
Spirit World (Smith), 70
Spiritual Churches, description of services, 3–9, 15-17, 60–61, 62, 63, 64–65, 119, 125–37; doctrine, 62, 68–71, 117; origin and development, 11, 13, 59–60, 72, 109–11
Spiritual Churches of New Orleans, The (Jacobs and Kaslow), 111
Spiritualist movement, 68–69, 77–78, 110–11, 116
Stillman, Isaiah, 40, 41
Stuckey, Sterling, 93
Superior Council, 88
Swaggart, Jimmy, 117
Sycamore Creek, 40

Tallant, Robert, 95–98, 102
Taylor, Zachary, 42

Tchoupitoulas, 106
Temple of the Innocent Blood, 13–14, 15, 73
Texas, 61, 65
Thompson, Robert Farris, 91, 92, 94
Thwaites, Reuben, 32
Treasure Street, 128
Trepagnier, Vincent, 107–08
Trinidad, 103
True Light compound. *See* Temple of the Innocent Blood
True Light Spiritualist Church, 119
Tunica Indians, 83
Turner, Katharine C., 43–44, 46, 48
Tyson, Dora, 58, 62, 63, 69–70, 95, 115, 118

Up From the Cradle of Jazz (Berry), 107

Venezuela, 103
Vicksburg, Mississippi, 78
Vieux Carré, 92
Virgin Mary. *See* Mary, Saint
Vodun, 90–91, 93, 95, 100
Voodoo, 19, 90–91, 92, 95–101, 102, 110, 114, 121, 122
Voodoo in New Orleans (Tallant), 95–98

Wallace, Anthony F. C., 27, 29, 30, 38–39
War of 1812, 32, 37, 41
Washington, Joseph, Jr., 116–17
Washington, D.C., 39, 41, 44
West Africa, 81–82, 90
West Indies, 80, 84